Beemasters of the Past

From: "Insect Manufactures" (1847)

Beemasters of the Past

by Victor Dodd
Illustrations by Jenny Brown

NORTHERN BEE BOOKS

NORTHERN BEE BOOKS

ISBN 978-1-904846-41-3

Printed 2009
Published by Northern Bee Books, Scout Bottom Farm, Mytholmroyd, Hebden Bridge, West Yorkshire, HX7 5JS.

Cover photograph:
William Herrod-Hempsall F.E.S.
Taken from Bee-Keeping, New & Old Described with Pen & Camera 1930

Acknowledgments.

I would like to thank those who have helped me in the preparation of this book.

In particular, Ruth and Jeremy Burbidge, whose faith and enthusiasm have helped to keep the wheels turning, and Mary Nash, who has not only typed the manuscript, but expunged the text of at least some of the worst lapses of grammar and style.

Some of the material has previously appeared in articles published in **Bee Craft, Beekeepers News, American Bee Journal**, and I would like to thank the respective editors for their co-operation and help. Tom Lloyd-Roberts, David Hughes, Tony Davies, Chris Baron and Dr. Stern have helped with books, as have the International Bee Research Association Library, and Karl Showier. I am also grateful for the encouragement and help of Dr. Eva Crane, The Director of I.B.R.A. whilst **British Bee Books: a bibliography**, (I.B.R.A.) was, of course, invaluable.

I make no apology for reproducing the chapter on Charles Butler as it appeared in **American Bee Journal** (June 1981), because in preparing this article I had, through the kind offices of the librarian of Magdalen College, Jasper Scovil, the good fortune to make contact with W. T. Butler, a descendant, and leading authority on his life. Both these gentlemen, although not beekeepers, provided sources of information which undoubtedly enriched the finished product. I am also indebted to David A. Smith, the Rev. J. C. Litton and R. T. Schadla-Hall. After publication, this article was instrumental in bringing to light an interesting essay on Butler, by Dr. G. E. Fussell, in Estate Magazine (July 1937), and I am grateful to the C.G.A., for enabling me, not only to have a copy for my own file, but to re-unite this distinguished historian with one of his long forgotten off-spring.

The British Bee Journal has been a useful source of material, and I wish to thank C. C. Tonsley for permisison to use this, as well as the signed portrait of T. W. Cowan. For the picture of Maurice Maeterlinck I am indebted to George Allen and Sons, and for Neighbour's to the Religious Society of Friends. Harry Wickens kindly loaned a snapshot of R. O. B. Manley, and B. V. Try, Steele and Brodie, and E. H. Thorne (Beehives) Ltd have helped in various ways.

Illustrations have been rather a problem because usually there is only one "likeness" available, and this is not always suitable for reproduction. It is hoped that the drawings of Jenny Brown, as well as providing a suitable apiarian atmosphere, will give a fair idea as to the appearance and character of those concerned. Her interest and enthusiasm for this formidable task is much appreciated.

Finally, my thanks to Harold Worthington, Leslie Thorne and especially to Harrison Ashforth, whose formidable knowledge and experience in this field has been invaluable; also to Bryn Williams, Ernie Cockeram and Douglas Albones, members of the North Clwyd Beekeepers' Association.

Contents

This book is dedicated to my brother,
John Gerald Dodd,
a natural scholar,
who was killed in action
on 29th May, 1942.

Preface

Many hundreds of books have been written about Bees and Beekeeping, spanning many centuries and emanating from many countries. Mostly, they concern methods whereby bees may be kept for the benefit of man, but there is also a considerable amount of purely scientific literature. In fact, no other insect or animal has stimulated the production of as many books and pamphlets as The Honey Bee.

The reason for this becomes apparent when one considers the part which bees have played in men's lives since the earliest times. Few products, for example, can have had such diverse applications as honey, not only as a source of food, but also in medicine, cosmetics, folk lore, and so on. In addition, royal jelly, bee venom, pollen and wax have all been extolled at various times as being the answer to some human problem.

Comparatively little has been written about the people who have devoted their time to the study of bees and the development of the craft. This seems to be a pity because they are often every bit as interesting as the work for which they are remembered. So, the aim of this book is not so much to trace the development of men's knowledge of Bees and Beekeeping, which has been done before, but more to highlight some of the men who have concerned themselves in this field.

As with music, it is an area where very few women have made much impression, at least until the present century, and in some cases little is known about the men. Obviously, rough boundaries have had to be set both in time and nationality. The seventeenth century seemed to make the most convenient starting point because the first specialist books began to appear at about that time. Many of these books were British; indeed, according to the Rev. Samuel Purchas, "The knowledge of bees was never truly communicated to the world by any but an Englishman." That was in 1657, however, and although books in the English language have out-numbered the others on this subject, it would be no justification for restricting our present interest to one country. So, whilst the bias will be towards the British contribution, and neither the Americans nor the Continentals will be entirely overlooked, there has to be some degree of selectivity. There have been several interesting Russian beemasters, for example, but works in that language are beyond the scope of this writer, and Dorothy Galton's Survey of a Thousand Years of Beekeeping in Russia, (B.R.A. 1971) is still readily available.

The basis throughout has been to use the writings of those concerned, as well as written comments about them by others. This leads to a false position, particularly in the recent past, where only those beekeepers who put pen to paper are likely to be considered as "beemasters." Nothing could be further from the truth, of course, and most people who have been interested in beekeeping for any length of time will have their own ideas as to who the real beemasters are!

It is a pity that no comprehensive history of the British Beekeepers' Association has been published since Cowan's in 1928, and no attempt is made here to cover this subject. Despite the fact that some beekeepers seem to live for ever, their work often spanning several generations, it has nevertheless been thought advisable not to include those who are still living, other than to mention one or two names for the sake of the narrative.

Finally, mention must be made of the excellent work done by Dr. H. Malcolm Fraser, particularly his book, History of Beekeeping in Great Britain. It was he who first charted this field, and if we are able to add a little more colour and detail to the framework he has provided, then others too may feel inclined to follow in his footsteps. Hopefully, these may include readers who have a general interest in our heritage, and not merely the loyal brotherhood of beekeepers.

Chapter One

BUTLER

SOLERTIA ET LABORE. SOLERTIA ET LABORE.
SOCORDIAM LVIMVS
Miraris Arte conditas mirâ domos,
Opesque regales in his reconditas?
SOLERTIA ET LABORE fiunt omnia.

From: "The Feminine Monarchie" (1609).

"In a word, thou must be chaste, cleanly, sweet, sober, quiet and familiar; so will they love thee, and know thee from all other".

Interest in history is sometimes stifled by school day memories. A slavish learning about events remote from modern life can easily become dry and boring, and may cauterise any feeling for the past from ever developing. This is a pity because history can be so pleasurable and absorbing, especially when assimilated out of natural curiosity, away from the compulsions, of an educational curriculum.

In a sense, we all live to some extent on past experience, and in maturity we perhaps become more willing to consider the lives of our forefathers, and the way they lived. Conditions change from generation to generation, of course, but human nature itself remains remarkably consistent, and therein lies much of the magnetism which draws us back into the past.

Consider the craft of beekeeping. It is only in the last hundred years or so that great advances in technology and scientific knowledge have taken place, but the products of the hive have not changed. These have been sought after for centuries, and to satisfy the demand for them men have, in one way or another, kept bees.

We can go back to the ancient civilisations and find that quite sound ideas as to how an apiary should be run had been formulated, but then we enter into a long, long period of many hundreds of years when very little is known about either the beekeepers or their methods.

Following the growth of printing, books on all manner of subjects began to circulate more widely, and eventually in 1609 a clergyman named Charles Butler published a book, **The Feminine Monarchie**, and it is this book and this man which mark the end of the so-called dark ages so far as beekeeping is concerned.

THE

FEMININE MONARCHIE

Or

A TREATISE CONCERNING BEES, AND THE DVE ORDERING OF THEM:

Wherein

The truth, found out by experience and diligent obſervation, diſcovereth the idle and fond conceipts, which many haue writ-ten anent this ſubiect.

By

CHAR: BVTLER Magd:

At Oxford,

Printed by Ioſeph Barnes. 1609.

It was not the first book in the English language on this subject, but in both style and content it stands out like a brilliant light at the end of a tunnel. Both the book and the man are worthy of our attention.

Charles Butler was essentially a scholar, but he was also a practising beekeeper of considerable ability. Previously, writers had leaned heavily on the often fanciful opinions of Virgil and others, whereas Butler gives us a complete system of practical beekeeping based on his own. experiences. The findings of others are measured against intensive personal observation, and whilst his conclusions may sometimes sound a little quaint to modern ears, in no way do they detract from the down-to-earth business of keeping bees.

Given a modicum of patience, the present day reader will find little difficulty in coping with the language in this delightful book. In no time at all he will feel himself in intimate touch with the seventeenth century, possibly more so than by any other means, such as old paintings, or buildings.' Early on it may help to read a few pages aloud, for the language of Butler derives from the same sources as the James I edition of the Bible, of Shakespeare and John Donne. It has the refreshing clarity of pure spring water, and because Butler is describing a practical subject, the absence of fanciful images and allusions avoids any feeling of obscurity.

Before looking more closely at **The Feminine Monarchie**, we should, perhaps, bear in mind that in Butler's time fancy and superstition were much more prevalent than factual knowledge, especially regarding natural history. Shakespeare, you will remember, wrote about the bees' thighs being packed with wax, and their mouths with honey. It was said that bees came forth from rotting cattle, and hornets from the carrion of horses. "They make among them a king," said one writer, "the most worthy in highness and fairness, and most clear in mildness, for that is the chief virtue in a king." Bees that were "Unobedient" to the king died by the wound of their own sting. "A bee's sting prickest deepest when it is fullest of honey." And so on.

Set against this background of old wives' tales, Butler's stature increases immeasurably. His book is arranged in the most orderly way, and there is no sign that he allowed himself to be influenced by anything other than firsthand knowledge. In fact, it has been rightly said that much of his instruction could still be profitably followed today, despite the radical differences in methods.

The beekeeping described by Butler was only really superseded when wooden hives with moveable frames were adopted, and this change did not gain much impetus until the nineteenth century. The bees were housed in skeps made of either straw or wicker, and these were generally placed on wooden stools; those of stone, said Butler, were too hot in hot weather, and which is worse, too cold in cold. He tells us how to dress the rough edges to make them smooth so that the bees would not be obliged to spend three or four days, sometimes a week together. scraping and gnawing as though they were mice in he hive. Straw hackles, rather like coolie hats, were often fitted for protection from the weather.

Early swarms, "before the blowing of the knapweed," were very highly valued - equal to a load of hay according to the old rhyme - but late ones "blackberry swarms" - were seldom any good. Swarm catching played an important part in the beekeeper's calendar and Butler accordingly deals with it very thoroughly. Once hived, the bees were then left to build comb which was attached to hazlewood bars inserted in the skep, and so established themselves.

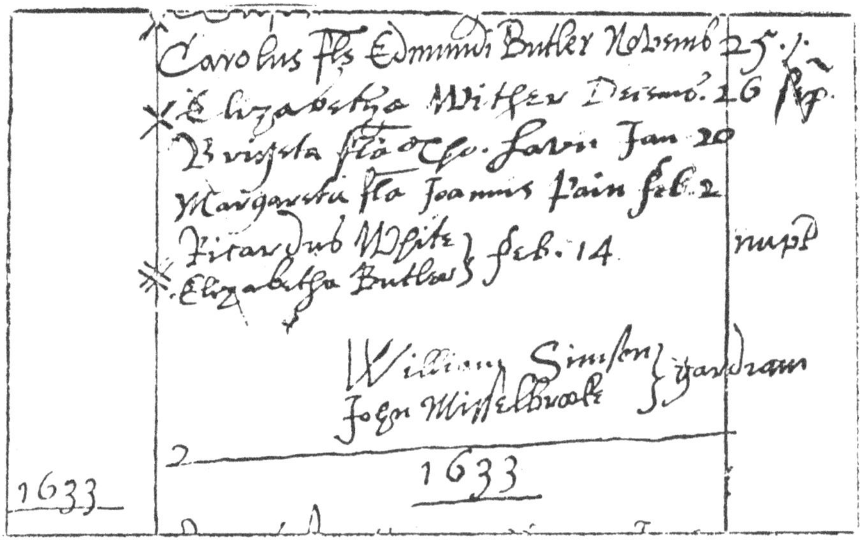
Carolus fils Edmundi Butler Novemb 25
Elizabetha Wither Decemb. 26
Brigitta filia Tho. Lavin Jan 20
Margareta filia Joannis Pain feb. 2
Richardus White } feb. 14 nupt
Elizabetha Butler }
William Simpson } Guardian
John Misselbrook }
1633
1633

Extract from Parish Register, Wootton St. Lawrence.

Late September was usually the best time for the taking of the honey by which time there would be less brood, "Neither do the bees any whit diminish the honey in their hives until the end of this month, unless much foul weather keep them long in before." Taking the honey meant killing the bees over a small pit of burning sulphur, or brimstone as it was called. Other kinds of smoke, such as that from damp straw, could be used but these usually contaminated the honey. Other methods such as driving or drowning were described, but these had many disadvantages. Usually, the older stocks which promised a good yield were selected, and any stock over five years old was not allowed to continue. A number of stocks had to be left as stores, and normally these would be the later swarms. Once the bees were dead, after about a quarter of an hour, the combs could be cut out and the honey, warmed if necessary, strained through a sieve.

This slaughter of the bees troubled the consciences of beekeepers for many years in a way which has never disturbed other livestock keepers. In some respects it was wasteful, of course, but many believe that the system helped to reduce disease.

Be that as it may, although skeps were much less costly to make than timber hives, they suffered numerous disadvantages. In hot weather, for example, combs were apt to melt, and thereby greatly increase the risk of robbing. Butler deals with this problem at length, even to the point of suggesting that at harvest time, when people are busy in The Fields, it was wise to leave somebody at home to watch. Only a man who had had experience of the nightmare of fighting bees, not to mention plagues of wasps, could have written so graphically and with so much feeling. Butler provides a fair description of the metamorphic development of bees, and although he was under the impression that the queen was somehow born instantly, he was in no doubt about her sex. Incidentally, it is interesting to note that Moses Rusden in his book, **A Further Discovery of Bees**, published seventy years later, always refers to the queen as "the King-bee".

From: British Bee Journal. Signature of Charles Butler.

From: third edition "The Feminine Monarchie" (1634).

Printed to enable four singers to use one book.

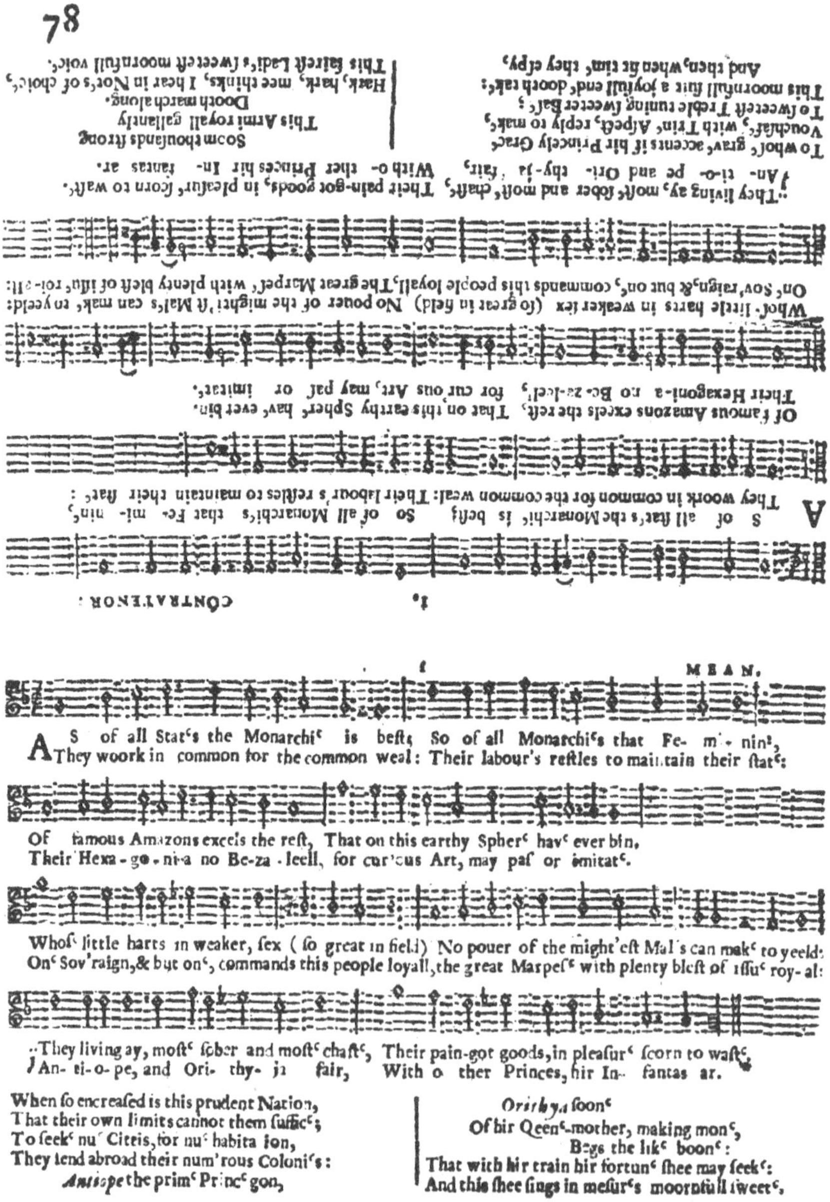

BASSUS.

A S of all stat's the monarchi' is best; So of all Monarchi's that Fe-mi-nin',
They woork in common for the common-weal: Their labour's restles to maintain their stat':

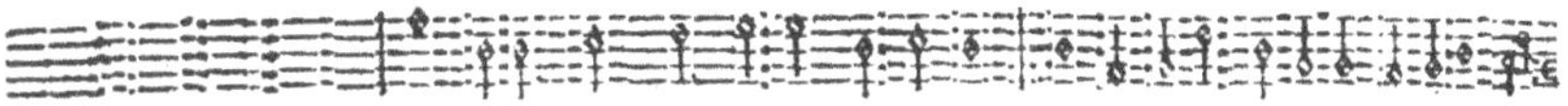

Of famous Amazons excels the rest, That on this earthy Spher' hav' ever bin.
Their Hexa-gonia no Be-za-leel, for cur'ous Art may pas' or imi-tate.

Whos' little harts in weaker sex (so great in field) No pouer of the might'st Mal's can mak' to yeeld:
On' Sov'raign, & but on', commands this people loyall, The great Marpes' with plenty blest of issu' roy-all:

They living ay, most' sober and most' chast', Their pain-got goods in pleasur' scorn to wast'.
An-ti-o-pe, and Ori-thy-ja fair, With o-ther Princes, hir In-fan-tas ar.

When so encreased is this prudent Nation,
That their own limits cannot them suffic';
To seek nu Citties, for nu habitation,
They send abroad their num'rous Colonies:
Antiope the prim' Princ' gon,
Orithya soon,
Of hir Qeen'-mother, making mon',
Begs the lik' boon:
That with hir train hir fortun' thee may seek;
And this thee sings in mesur's moornfull sweet.

79

TENOR

I

A S of all stat's the Monarchi' is best; So of all Monarchi's that Fe- mi- nin',
They woork in common for the common weal: Their labour's restles to maintain their stat':

Of famous Amazons excels the rest, That on this earthy Spher' hav' ever bin.
Their Hexa- gonia no Beza- leel, for cur'ous Art, may pas' or imitat',

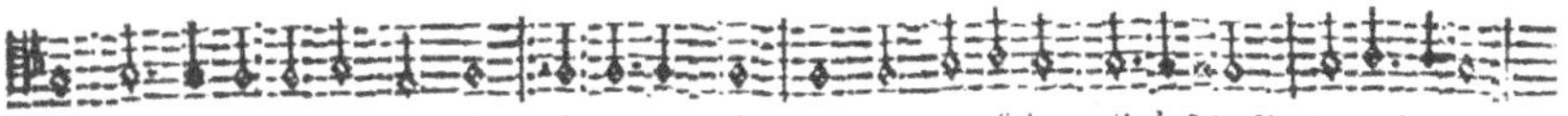

Whos' little harts in weaker sex (so great in field) No pouer of the might'est Mal's Can mak' to yeeld:
On' Sov'raign, & but on', commands this people loyall, The great Marpes' with plenty blest of issu' roy- all:

They living ay, most' sober and most' chast', Their pain-got goods in pleasur' scorn to wast'.
An- ti- o- pe, and O- ri- thy- ja fair, With o- ther Princes, hir In- fan- tas ar.

To whos' grav' accents if her Princ'ly Grac'
Vouchsafe, with Trine Aspect, reply to make,
To sweetest Treble tuning sweeter Base;
This moornfull suit a joyfu'l ende dooth take:
And then, when fit time they espy,

Soom thousands strong,
This Armie royall gallantly
Dooth march along.
Hark, hark, mee thinks, I hear in Notes of choice,
This fairest Ladies sweetest moornfull voice.

No reader of **The Feminine Monarchie** can fail to be impressed by Butler's sense of observation, or by the systematic way in which he records information. His whole guarded and careful approach was later echoed in the work of Francis Huber, and it is perhaps significant that both these men are somehow able to communicate a special sense of revelation in their writings. One has only to study Butler's accounts of the wasp and the bumble-bee to realise what a good naturalist he was. Charles Butler also had a very good ear for music, and towards the end of his long life he published, **The Principles of Music**, (1636). This was the only theoretical work on music published in the reign of King Charles I, and it is perhaps not surprising that he related his musical knowledge to the sound of bees. In the first edition of **The Feminine Monarchie** Butler gives a proper musical notation, written on a four line stave, of various bee sounds at swarming time. "But the Queen in a deeper voice thus, ... " (followed by the notation) "continuing the same, some four or five semibreves and sounding the end of every note in C ... ". In the third edition (1634), Butler went still further by writing a four part madrigal, using a five line stave. This "bee music" was performed by students from Oxford when a stained glass window to his memory was unveiled at the parish church of Wootton St. Lawrence, Hampshire, where he was vicar for forty-seven years. Fittingly, Dr. H. Malcolm Fraser, the distinguished beekeeper-historian performed the ceremony, which took place on the 14th November, 1954.

The fact that **The Feminine Monarchie** ran to three editions in his lifetime is a measure of the book's success, and the third edition is particularly interesting because it brings out yet another facet of this remarkable man's career. Butler was very conscious of the difficulties of spelling in the English Language, and in his book, **The English Grammar**, (1633), he sets out a new orthography for the language. In essence, it is a system of phonetic spelling, and in order to demonstrate its use, he must have had to revise the whole of the text for the publication of this edition of **De Feminin Monarki**, (The actual 'D' was printed with a bar across to convey the "TH" sound). Although it is not impossible for the modern reader, the first edition, which is the one which has been reprinted in facsimile, is certainly easier to follow. The system was perhaps too drastic for it to be generally adopted, but it was important enough for Samuel Johnson to comment upon when he published his famous dictionary over a hundred years later. It has attracted the attention of many scholars since.

The third edition was dedicated to Queen Henrietta Maria and so set a vogue for bee books to be dedicated to queens rather than kings. (Wildman to Queen Charlotte, Warder to Queen Anne, Bevan to Queen Victoria, but Rusden to King Charles II).

Sufficient has perhaps been said to demonstrate that Charles Butler was a man with substantial intellectual powers, but it would be wrong to see him as a clergyman who spent most of his time immersed in books, closeted in the vicarage adjacent to Wootton church, emerging only to attend his bees when the weather was fair. There is no doubt that he carried out the duties of a parish priest as conscientiously as any; repairs to the fabric of the church, baptisms, marriages and burials are all recorded in the registers in his own neat hand. Four of the six bells which hang in the belfry at Wootton were installed during Butler's time, and as with many rural clergymen of the period, he did a little farming. He must have done at least some of The Field work himself because, when describing a honey flow, he says, "The bees are exceeding earnest plying their business like me in harvest." Certainly he was knowledgeable about the making of mead and metheglin for he describes these activities in such detail as could only have come from hands which had many times done this work. In this same way, he knew, not only about the problems of honey extraction, but also the making of preserves, and the numerous medical purposes for which honey could be used. As regards wax, he believed it to be gathered by the bees, although the extraction and refinement of it was no problem to him. But listen to these words about honey:

> "In cold weather the honey will not work well without the heat of the fire. The best way is to put it into an oven after the batch is forth, but not before you can abide to hold your hand upon the bottom, for fear of over heating the honey".

Hardly anything seems to be known about Butler's early days, and there is even some uncertainty about his date of birth. Despite conflicting evidence, the most likely date for this appears to be 1560. His entry to Magdalen Hall, Oxford, at the age of eighteen was due to academic promise, rather than to wealth or influence. In 1579, he entered Magdalen College as a chorister, one of about sixteen students whose duties included waiting at table. Most of Butler's fellow students came from influential families, although quite a number of "poor scholars" were accepted in order to enhance the reputation of the college; already this had been high enough to justify a visit from Queen Elizabeth I some years before Butler's time.

Life in college was by no means harsh; conversation had to be in Latin, but there was little pressure and some of the students lived idly and ended up, according to an official visitor, as "ignorant ministers or rogues." Deer stealing was not unknown, and in 1586 one student was put in jail for this offence. The apparent harshness of this sentence caused quite a serious riot; fighting occured around the Bear Inn and showers of stones were hurled from the

College Tower. The offenders were subsequently punished, and some were expelled. Charles Butler, however, was not among them, and the following year he became a Master of Arts, six years after matriculation.

From: first edition "The Feminine Monarchie" (1609).

C.5. *Of the ſwarming of Bees*

great and timely ſwarmes. But if the ſtall be
of many yeeres, then turning the bottome of
the hiue vpward ſet a leere prepared hiue faſt
vpon it:into which they wil aſcend and worke
and breed there as well as in the old. At *Libra*
v.c.10. par. you may driue *v.* them all into the new hiue,
1.n.17. and take the old for your labour.

21 *The ſignes of after ſwarms* The ſignes of the after-ſwarmes are more
certaine. For whereas the riſing of the prime-
ſwarme is appointed by the vncertaine vulgar,
whoſe chiefe direction is the fulnes of the hiue,
the hiue being now well emptied, for other

22 ſwarmes there needeth ſome other warning,
The riſing of the after-ſwarmes is appointed by the rulers which the rulers themſelues doe giue by their
voices:without which that ſtock will ſwarme
no more that yeere. And yet the choice of the
hower, yea and of the day among foure or fiue
is permitted vnto them, as beſt knowing the
diſpoſition of the weather.

23 *When they begin to call or ſing.* When the prime-ſwarme is gon(if the ſtock
ſhal ſwarme any more) the ſeauenth or eight
euening after, ſomtime the ninth, tenth, or ele-
uenth, the next prince, when ſhe perceiueth a
competent number to be fledge and ready,
beginneth the muſick in a begging tune, as if
ſhe did pray hir queen-mother to let them go:
whereunto if ſhe yeeld conſent by hir anſwering (as to the petition of hir ſecond daughter
ſhe ſeldome ſaith nay, though ſometime ſhee
conſent not in two or three daies) then looke
for

He continued at Oxford until 1593, when he became vicar of the tiny, early Norman church at Nately Scures, in Hampshire. According to Anthony Wood's **Athenae Oxonienses** (1691), this was a poor preferment for such a worthy

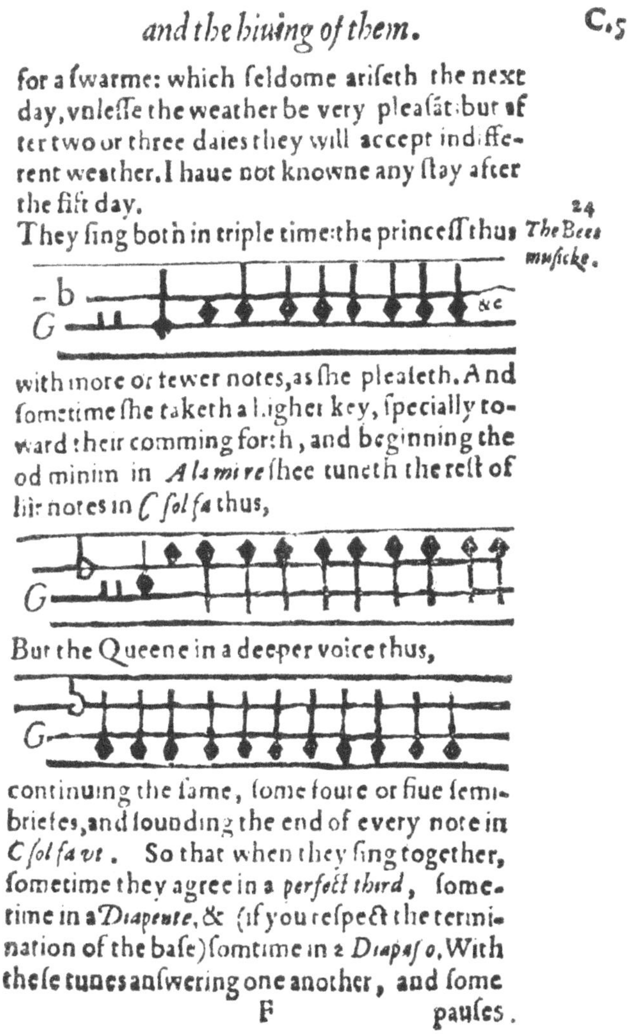

and the hiuing of them. C.5

for a ſwarme: which ſeldome ariſeth the next day, vnleſſe the weather be very pleaſāt: but af ter two or three daies they will accept indiffe- rent weather. I haue not knowne any ſtay after the fift day.

They ſing both in triple time: the princeſſ thus 24 *The Bees muſicke.*

with more or fewer notes, as ſhe pleaſeth. And ſometime ſhe taketh a higher key, ſpecially to- ward their comming forth, and beginning the od minim in *Alamire* ſhee tuneth the reſt of hir notes in *C ſol fa* thus,

But the Queene in a deeper voice thus,

continuing the ſame, ſome foure or fiue ſemi- briefes, and ſounding the end of every note in *C ſol fa vt*. So that when they ſing together, ſometime they agree in a *perfect third*, ſome- time in a *Diapente*, & (if you reſpect the termi- nation of the baſe) ſomtime in a *Diapaſo*. With theſe tunes anſwering one another, and ſome

F pauſes.

scholar. Shortly afterwards, he was appointed schoolmaster at the Fraternity of the Holy Ghost, four miles away at Basingstoke, no doubt to supplement a meagre living. Nowadays, only the ruins of this school remain, but a plaque to Butler's memory stands on a wall there. Incidentally, this was the school attended by the naturalist, Gilbert White, author of **Natural History of Selbourne** (1789), and this may have led to a misunderstanding that Gilbert White was a descendant of Charles Butler. In fact, Gilbert was a descendant of Sir Sampson White, whose brother, Richard, married Butler's daughter, Elizabeth. Nevertheless, the association of both Gilbert White and Charles Butler with the Basingstoke School is interesting.

Butler seems to have been a good schoolmaster, and it is during this period that he wrote **Rhetoric Libri** (1600), a successful book on logic which ran to at least four editions, and was widely used in schools and colleges. He was probably married at this time, and he would almost certainly have kept some hives of bees at Nately Scures.

On the 17th November, 1600, the Bishop of Winchester installed Charles Butler as vicar of the small parish of Wootton St. Lawrence, and the question arises as to why such an able person did not progress further into the higher echelons of the Church, The authorities may not have been particularly impressed by **The Feminine Monarchie**, despite its orderly arrangement and excellent style, but a few years later, Butler wrote another masterly work dealing with affinity as a bar to marriage, which was also widely acclaimed in many quarters. He ran his parish well, and was a good father to his children, even to the extent of presenting his daughter Elizabeth, "the honey girl", with some hives of bees upon her marriage! Incidentally, this dowry is sometimes valued at £400 which seems to be a gross exaggeration. How could such a patently able man have been overlooked?

To answer this question it may perhaps help to glance briefly at the conditions under which he lived. The church at that time was very much an instrument of the Government and religion was bound up with politics. Advancement depended on having influence in the right places, and Butler did not have that kind of influence. On the other hand, it may well be that he was content to lead a scholarly life in a rural setting. It was the pulpit which provided the means whereby the government communicated with the people, and it was, for example, because Catholicism was based in countries antagonistic to the State that it suffered persecution, not primarily because of religious differences. Politics are about power, and the church was a necessary instrument in its exercise. The bishops, too, had great powers, and in 1610, for example, one of the mildest of them caused a Catholic monk to be hanged, drawn and quartered for saying mass at a clandestine meeting in London. Similarly, the rise of the Puritans, of which Butler must have been more than well aware, was partly due to the overbearing way in which tithes were gathered by the Church, rather than because candles were placed on altars. The great political problems, both both national and international, were inextricably woven into a religious background, and even in a book such as **The Feminine Monarchie** there is evidence of the way in which such matters reverberated in a small community such as Wootton St. Lawrence.

In the final chapter of the first edition, (it was omitted from the third), Charles Butler becomes a different man, incensed by what he felt to be an injustice. Throughout the book, Butler is like a generous host showing us good-naturedly round his warm and friendly house, but as we come into the last room, the whole atmosphere changes. "Thus have I disclosed unto thee the hidden secrets of the bees and their fruits. Now ... be thankful unto God and pay justly the tithe." Then follows a powerful sermon in which, using the most stringent language, Butler pleads for the proper payment of tithes to the Church. "Bring ye all the tithes into the storehouse that there may be meat in mine house." People were now questioning the centuries-old tradition whereby a tenth of the produce of a parish was paid in kind to the church. Also, it was becoming more difficult to administer the tithes because methods of farming were changing, other industries were developing, and furthermore, the market-places were plagued by inflation.

Butler, already at a disadvantage by having but a modest parish, found it far from easy to make ends meet, for the clergy had had little increase in stipends since their days of celibacy. He presents a convincing case, but the turmoil over tithes was to continue for many years, ~and in 1647 when he died, the ferment which could have brought him little peace in his declining years has boiled over into civil war.

Butler's body was laid to rest in an unmarked grave in the chancel of the parish church. At the age of 88 he had lived much longer than most of his contemporaries, thereby perhaps confirming what many writers since have pointed out, that beekeeping prolongs an active life!

Charles Butler has been called "the father of British Beekeeping," and indeed his name has been kept alive more by beekeepers than any, but he has left us more than an excellent account of beekeeping in his day. **The Feminine Monarchie** has the same warm-hearted quality which endears us to Langstroth and other classic writers in this field. To read these books helps us to know the men, and in the case of Charles Butler this is a particularly pleasant experience.

Chapter Two

Evelyn, Gedde

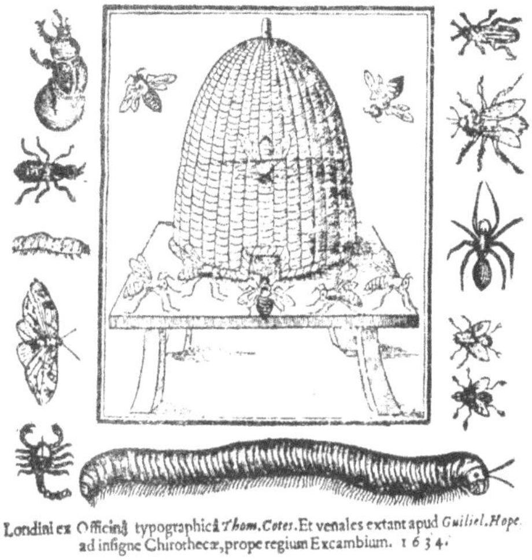
Londini ex Officinâ typographicâ Thom. Cotes. Et venales extant apud Guiliel. Hope
ad insigne Chirothecæ, prope regium Excambium. 1634.

From: "Insectorum" by Thomas Mouffet (1634).

Charles Butler was not the first man to write a book entirely about bees. In 1593, Edmunde Southerne published, **A Treatise Concerning the Right Use and Ordering of Bees**. Nothing appears to be known about Southerne, apart from the fact that he was a practical beekeeper. His book, like Butler's, ends on the subject of tithes, and the story about a beekeeper being called upon to deliver his tenth swarm to the parson is included in W. C. Cotton's **My Bee Book**.

The beekeeper said he would willingly give up one tenth of his honey and wax to the parson, but not the bees.

"Tythe bees!" protested the beekeeper, "I never yet paid any, neither is it the custom of this parish, and I am loth to be the first that shall bring it up. and yet I am very willing to pay my due; honey and wax you shall have with all my heart; but bees cannot be told (counted), therefore how shall I pay them?"

"Told, or told not," replied the parson, "or due or due not, I will have the tenth swarm, and you were best bring them home to my house. "

"Why, then, I might deceive you," said the beekeeper, and bring you a castling or an after swarm for a whole swarm."

"Never mind, the honey money and wax shall make amends for that, so bring me the bees. "

Two days later the beekeeper had a heavy swarm, and towards nightfall carried them in a skep to the parson's house. He found the parson having supper with his family, and touching his cap politely, said; "I've brought you some bees." "This is neighbourly done," replied the parson with a smile, "would you carry them into the garden?"

"Nay, by troth," said the beekeeper. "I will leave them here!" With that, he gave the skep a knock against the ground, and the bees were released: "some stung the parson, some stung his wife, and some his children and family; and out they ran as fast as they could into a chamber, and well was he who could make shift for himself, leaving their meate upon the table in the hall. The gentleman went home carrying his emptie hive with him. On the next morning the bees were found in a quickset hedge by a poore man, who since hath made good profit of them, and is yet living".

In the normal way, bees are not aggressive creatures, but over the years stories are not uncommon whereby a beekeeper has utilised fierce bees, either wittingly or otherwise, to his own advantage. There was the smallholder in Victorian times, for instance, who kept his bees behind the hedge leading up to his house, and when the tithe gatherers came, would up-turn his most aggressive hive, and so send the unwelcome callers away.

Potentially, of course, any hive of bees has the power to kill a man, but the number, of fatalities due to bees is minute. This may be one of the reasons why the stealing of bees has been as common down the ages as sheep-stealing, and has never died out. Charles Butler had some strong words about these "base, cowardly knaves, neither fit for labour or service: a burden to the Commonwealth, and as incorrigable as sheep-biting curs, which being once fleshed do seldom desist."

> "Whose keep weel sheeps and Bee'n
> Sleep, or wake, their thrift comes in"

As a rule, books to do with agriculture contain little or nothing about bees, but during the seventeenth century particularly there were a number of exceptions. A contemporary of Butler, Gervaise Markham, published, **Cheape and Good Husbandry for the Well Ordering of all Beast and Fowles**, in 1614. This was a popular book which appeared in several guises, and although the bee content was relatively small, Markham himself was quite an interesting character. He wrote on horsemanship and military matters, as well as gardening and agriculture. He also wrote poetry, plays and a novel so that, although he described himself as a "great master of these creatures, neither have I spared to bestow my pen in the advancement of the art at knowledge of the bee," Markham is unusual in his wide range of subjects. Most of the beemasters wrote only about bees, often only a single work, although there are many exceptions, of course, and this is perhaps why Markham is sometimes thought of, perhaps unfairly, as the first hack writer on bees.

Richard Remnant, Samuel Hartib and John Worlidge all wrote about husbandry in one form or another, as well as about bees during this period. Hartlib was the son of a Polish merchant, and a friend of the poet John Milton. He was not a beekeeper, but his book, **The Reformed Commonwealth of Bees**" (1665), gives the earliest known description of the octagonal three-storied hive designed by the Rev. W. Mew, of Gloucestershire, and includes a drawing by Sir Christopher Wren.

Of course, by no means all those who have contributed to the development of beekeeping have themselves been beekeepers. For instance, Samuel Purchas wrote **A Theatre of Political Flying-insects** in 1657, and a traveller, Sir George Wheeler, in his book **A Journey into Greece** (1682), described skeps with moveable bars. This was probably the first reference to a principle which was to become one of the main elements in modern beekeeping.

Again, descriptions of beekeeping are sometimes found in unexpected places. In 1681 **The Young Man's Companion**, a manual giving easy directions for spelling, reading and writing English" ... with easy rules for arithmetic and the Englishing of the Latin Bible," contained a section on the ordering of bees. This book by William Mather ran through many editions, but by 1737, the section on bees had been dropped. A similar book with the same title, but under a different publisher, and author, was published with quite a lengthy section on beekeeping in 1814, and there were others.

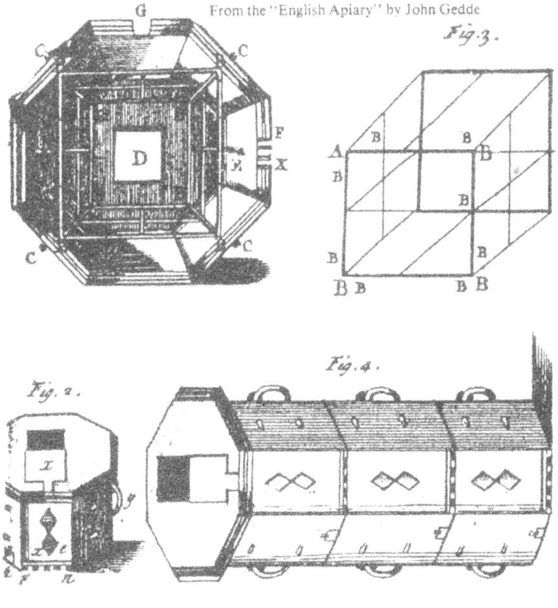

From the "English Apiary" by John Gedde

It may come as a mild surprise to some to find that the famous diarist, John Evelyn, was a beekeeper. Evelyn was a friend of Samuel Pepys, also the poet John Dryden. He held a number of public appointments, and wrote prolifically on various subjects. His lifelong interest was gardening, and there are many references to bees in his **Kalandarium hortense, or the Gardener's Almanac** (1664). John Evelyn was an early member of the Royal Society, which was founded in 1660, and when the commissioners of the navy became concerned about the depletion of standing timber, they referred a number of queries to the society. Evelyn became involved in dealing with these matters, and eventually published his best known work **Sylva** (1664), on the subject. It was hoped that this book would encourage landowners in the planting and preservation of trees for the benefit of the nation.

The formation of the Royal Society was an expression of the growth of interest in scientific progress and, as we shall see later, the influence of John Evelyn in beekeeping matters was probably greater than is generally realised.

Whilst it may be dangerous, perhaps downright foolish, to generalise about beekeepers, it is nevertheless interesting to consider a few aspects of Evelyn's life and character which have been mirrored in his successors. Like Huber, Langstroth and many lesser figures, Evelyn was essentially an amiable character, "sweet, studious and high principled ... unfitted for the rough struggles of partisanship," as one biographer describes him. Without duplicity, he apparently managed to steer a peaceful course through a particularly turbulent period of history, and still remain respected. He went with arms and horse to join the army of Charles I, just after the battle of Brentford, but when, a few days later, the army moved to Gloucester, Evelyn returned to the family estates near London, afraid they would suffer depredation by his absence.

Or was it that he had no stomach to be a soldier? He went abroad, and married the daughter of Sir R. Brown, Charles I's minister at the French court. On their return, the couple lived at Sayes Court in Kent, which belonged to his father-in-law. Later, when the estate was confiscated, Evelyn was permitted to buy it. His ability to retain friends in the court of Cromwell, whilst retaining his royalist sympathies suggests a remarkably subservient nature. He lived to the age of 86.

Another aspect of John Evelyn's character, one which has taken varying forms in other beekeepers, is the impulse to embark on ambitious schemes beyond their capabilities. In Evelyn's case, he planned a massive work, **Elysium Britannicum**, which was to be a book on horticulture in three volumes, and, in fact, he actually completed some nine hundred pages, but by 1699 he realised that he would never finish the work. Much of the manuscript was lost, with only the first three hundred and forty-two pages surviving, and in 1965, David A.

Smith edited the section dealing with bees, and published it for the first time in **Bee World**. In 1966 the manuscript was published in the form of a booklet with an introduction and notes by the (International) Bee Research Association.

John Evelyn's work on bees was largely a hatch-patch of other peoples' ideas, and had it been published in his lifetime, it probably would not have made any great impression, except perhaps as the work of a "man of quality." Nevertheless, it is interesting that Mr. Smith 'has been able to identify a number of the sources which Evelyn used.

It seems certain, on the other hand, that Evelyn had an indirect influence on the beekeeping of his time. This came about because of his membership of the Royal Society, and as a result of his friendship with Charles II, who was the society's patron. His diary for 24th November, 1661, reads:

"This night his Majestie fell into discourse with me concerning bees, etc" .

The king also visited Evelyn's famous garden at Sayes Court "on purpose to see and contemplate with much satisfaction" the ornamental hives. Another visitor to this "lovely, noble ground" was Samuel Pepys who, in his diary (1665), mentions that, after dinner with Mr. Evelyn, he was shown a hive of bees which had glass windows. "You may see the bees making their honey and combs mighty pleasantly," he remarks. On the 21st July, 1673, the Royal society printed an account of bee boxes. This account has been provided by Sir Robert Murray, who had received it from Sir William Thomson. Now, neither of these gentlemen had any authority for the publishing of this work, because a practical beekeeper by the name of John Gedde claimed that the ideas were his. In his book **The English Apiary, or the Complete Beemaster**" (1675), Gedde explained that the information had been sent to Sir William Thomson privately, and was not intended for publication.

In all events, the publicity did Gedde no harm, and he succeeded in getting not only an acknowledgement from the Royal Society that the work was his, but also the patronage of "persons of quality." On 23rd April, 1675, John Gedde took out the first patent for a beehive, in the name of himself and his partners. No doubt they believed that they were on the threshold of commercial success, but as others found subsequently, it is one thing to take out a patent, and quite another to carry it through to fruition. The patent was for fourteen years.

The prospects must have seemed uncommonly good. Had not the King himself seen honey being taken without troubling the bees, and become convinced that if sufficient of his subjects could be persuaded to take up the craft, poverty and want could be greatly reduced? Gedde was given a grant of £200, and some land in order "to stir up such interest ... for the good and benefit of his whole subjects, rich and poor ... " This official support, possibly

Frontispiece of "Apiarium" by John Worlidge

APIARIUM;

OR A

DISCOURSE

OF

BEES:

Tending to the beſt Way of IMPROVING them, and to the Diſcovery of the Fallacies that are impoſed by ſome, for private Lucre, on the Credulous Lovers and Admirers of theſe Inſects.

Written by *J. W.* Gent.

LONDON,
Printed for and Sold by *Thomas Dring*
Bookſeller, at the Sign of the Harrow
at *Chancery*-lane-end in *Fleet-ſtreet*.
MDCLXXVI.

Title Page of "Apiarium" by John Worlidge

influenced by the fact that John Gedde had fought for the King at the Battle of Dunbar in 1650, certainly seemed to augur well.

As to the hive itself, it consisted of octagonal timber boxes which were kept in a bee house, which was made either of "wood, bricks or stone," covered with "lead, tile or thatch." Whilst theoretically promising, it was never a great success. The shape, incidentally, is thought to have been chosen as being the nearest one practicable to the winter cluster. It was by no means original, but was based on the design by the Rev. W. Mew, mentioned previously.

Gedde's book, on the other hand, was successful and ran to four editions, the latest being 1721. He believed that swarming, other than for planned increase was, as he put it, "discouraging to the owner and consumed his profit." He maintained that it was stupid to destroy the bees in order to take the honey. His belief that hives needed to be built up vertically in seperate compartments conformed with the concept that a hive should be capable of being expanded or contracted according to conditions. Gedde also understood that the provision of more space was a factor in swarm prevention, and he condemned the creating of a noise (tanging) as a means of persuading a swarm to settle. His comments about robbing, pests, feeding and the siting of the apiary are full of the commonsense to be expected from a practical beekeeper.

As with many writers, Gedde was by no means short of confidence. He promised to unfold "The whole art and mystery of the management of bees, and to collect and improve the work of all authors relating to this subject, ancient as well as modern." His "new discovery of an excellent method for making bee houses," was clearly intended as the final solution to the contentious problem of housing bees. Furthermore, he undertook "to free the owners from that great charge and trouble that attends the swarming of bees."

So, this canny Scotsman from Fyfe, the first businessman-beekeeper, with men of substance as partners, the patronage of the King and the interest of the Royal Society behind him, seemed all set to take advantage of an almost virgin market. On the face of it, John Gedde's fame and fortune seemed assured, and eventually, perhaps, his final place of rest might even be in Wren's great new cathedral!

Gedde was an old man when he died, over seventy, and certainly not wealthy, but when or where he died is not recorded. His expectations were never realised, and his critics were probably right when they said that many of his ideas were ill-founded and based on too little experience. Both J. W. Worlidge, mentioned earlier. and Dr. Robert Plot (**Natural History of Oxfordshire**, 1677) were among those who attacked Gedde's pretensions, and many felt that his patent inhibited the development of better hives. Gedde's hives were obviously much more expensive than straw skeps, and the cost of five or six pounds did not "abundently over-balance" their inconvenience, or advance the profit of the beekeeper, as he claimed.

Aside from these considerations, it should be remembered that conditions were not particularly conducive for commercial enterprise. London had but recently suffered both plague and fire, and even the travelling necessary to promote his ideas was a slow and hazardous business.

On the death of Charles II, Gedde applied for the renewal of his patent, but this time he was required to take certain oaths and to make a yearly payment of twenty pounds of wax. Whilst he did not altogether object to the payment of wax, he adamantly refused to take the oaths. The 'consequence was that the authorities made his life so difficult that he was obliged to take his family out of the country for a time.

Not surprisingly, John Gedde was not the only beekeeper who saw the business potential in the improvements now being advanced. There was an apothecary, named Moses Rusden, who lived in Westminster. He, too, saw the advantages to be gained by keeping in with the Royal Society, "the princes of virtue and knowledge," as he describes its members. In fact, his book **A Further Discovery of Bees**, 1679, was published by "His Majesty's especial command and approved by the Royal Society at Gresham College." Furthermore, almost as if to upstage Gedde, he describes himself as 'Beemaster to the King's most excellent Majesty."

As to Gedde's patent, Moses Rusden simply obtained a licence from John Gedde and his partners, made modifications of his own, and got on with the business of selling beehives. It seems doubtful, however, whether he made much of a success of it either, although his book enjoyed a popularity similar to Gedde's.

One interesting feature of Rusden's book is that The Queen Bee is always referred to as the king, and the inference is sometimes made that Rusden was a beekeeper of little consequence because of this misunderstanding; more especially, of course, because Charles Butler had been so clear on the point years earlier. The fact is that until the whole life-cycle of the honeybee had been thoroughly clarified, many years later, there was still room for intelligent men to put forward their conjectures. Moses Rusden sets out his case quite well, and the fact that he drew the wrong conclusions-as others were to do later-should not reflect him in an inferior light. Others have suggested that he did so for political reasons, and there are indeed a number of references to loyalty to the king, obedience, and so on, but there seems to be no real foundation for this assertion. Naturally, his title of Bee-master to the king gave rise to a certain amount of jealousy, and doubts about this appellation persisted long after his death. Now, thanks to the publication of John Evelyn's work, its authenticity has been finally established, although but for their books, both Rusden and Gedde would have long since been forgotten.

Chapter Three

SWAMMERDAM

"The Book of Nature" by Swammerdam

Nowadays, we take the rapid communication of information for granted. Had this been so in the days of Moses Rusden, he would not have doubted that The Queen Bee was truly female, because about that time a Dutchman named Jan Swammerdam had become the first man to dissect a bee, and in doing so established beyond doubt the sex of the Queen.

The foundation of the Royal Society by John Wilkins, later to become Bishop of Chester had been an important step towards a wider dissemination of knowledge. A number of papers were published relating to bees in the Society's transactions, the first of which was a review of Robert Hooke's **Micrographia**, a book containing a description and drawings of a bee's sting. This was the first study of an internal organ of the bee made with the aid of a microscope. Other papers included accounts of the work done by Goedartius, Leeuwenhoek, as well as Swammerdam. Incidentally, apart from members of the Royal Society already mentioned in the previous Chapter-Evelyn, Murray and Thompson-it is interesting to find that John Wilkins had also kept bees. Despite this interest by the Royal Society the communication of new ideas remained a slow and laborious process.

For example, Swammerdam's considerable work on insects was completed by about 1670, but nothing about his work on bees published in the first edition of **Historia insectorum generalis** (1669). It was not until 1737 when **Biblia natura** appeared that the material on bees became available, and a further twenty years were to elapse before the version in English, **The Book of nature** (1758), was published in London.

Now, although not a beemaster in the strictest sense the subject of Jan Swammerdam is worthy of our attention. It may perhaps incidentally help to identify the fever which sometimes draws men towards bees, beyond the bounds of normal scientific enquiry, or the harvest of honey for profit. Why men turn to beekeeping, for example, when their effort and expertise might bring them much greater material rewards in other channels. Why men sometimes turn to bees as a means of achieving, for the want of a better expression, "peace of mind."

Tolstoy, for instance, a writer with unparalleled insight into human nature, was a man from a well-to-do background who turned towards the soil in later life and in so doing became a beekeeper. Maeterlinck, the Belgian writer (see chapter X) became obsessed with bees, and sought to relate their organisation within the hive to the state of mankind. Was it something about the life-style of the peasant, and his supposed tranquility which attracted these restless, over driven minds? Or was it simply the spell of the honeybee?

Whatever the answers, neither Tolstoy or Maeterlinck found lasting contentment from their bees, and like Swammerdam, they spent their final years in misery. In the case of Swammerdam his interest in bees came in the final phase of a short life of intense mental and physical activity. After spending five years studying the honeybee, he did no further word of any kind, and whilst there were other influences at work, it is nevertheless noteworthy that bee research was instrumental in his breakdown. According to many, it was also his finest achievement.

J. Swammerdam

Swammerdam's schedule of work was almost terrifying by any normal standard. To make the most of the light, he would start work at six in the morning and when the light failed, he continued working far into the night making drawings and writing up the accounts of his experiments. Using microscopes of the simplest kind, he not only made special knives and scissors which could only be sharpened under magnification, he also developed his own techniques for filling the smallest veins with air, and tracing their paths with coloured fluids or wax. He also pioneered ways of preserving specimens, using alcohol and balsam. His drawings of the bees' anatomy, the mechanism of the sting and the intestines, for example, were almost perfect and scarcely improved upon for hundreds of years.

Despite these considerable achievements, and his confirmation that the queen was the sole mother of the colony, the bees' mode of reproduction escaped him. "I do not believe the male bees actually copulate with the female," he wrote. Nevertheless, he was thoroughly systematic in a programme of research which covered a massive spectrum of insect life. In a period of about sixteen years, he collected some 3,000 anatomical specimens, and was able to record the development of the insect from the egg.

Now, here was a man immersed in a totally absorbing subject, who must have been aware that he was successfully expanding the frontiers of knowledge, and yet his personal life was clouded by instability. Far from being uplifted by the excitement of discovery, or the satisfaction of work well done, he was tortured by doubt and insecurity. Swammerdam's interest in natural history had been stimulated by his father, an apothecary who possessed an unusual collection of curiosities. This museum was something of a show-piece in Amsterdam, and it attracted many visitors, including royalty. The boy took a great interest in this collection, and by the age of twelve had commenced his own collection of insects. Eventually, in 1651, he was sent to Leyden University to study medicine.

In the course of his studies, he became interested in anatomy, and his abilities brought him into contact with several leading anatomists of the day, including Nicholas Steno, and de Graff. He was also befriended by an influential French aristocrat, Thevionot, who arranged that he be given permission to dissect any patients "who happened to die" in Amsterdam hospital.

But, although he qualified as a doctor, he never practised medicine. Time was spent in France with both Thevionot and Steno, and he continued to dissect and investigate. both human and insect specimens. His abiding interest, however, proved to be insects. By the time he had reached the age of thirty, he showed no sign that he ever intended to earn his living in the and Swammerdam's father became concerned about his future. He was in no position to go on supporting a son who seemed to work only to please himself, and relations between the two deteriorated quite seriously.

Seeking to appease his father, Swammerdam promised to work as a doctor, and in the meantime set about the laborious task of cataloguing his father's extensive collection. Aware of the difficult situation, Thevionot offered Swammerdam facilities for study in France, but his father who made him an allowance of 400 guilders a year, refused to allow him to go.

Eventually, the strain became intolerable, and Jan Swammerdam went off to live in the country where he was able to devote his whole time to research. He read widely, and became fascinated by the works of Antoinette Bourignon, a religious reformist who had rejected organised religion in the belief that she was directly and uniquely inspired by God. Swammerdam's attitudes changed, and he now saw his own work as the examination of the works of God, pursued as a result of "the insatiable ambition which makes men desirous of superiority over others," whereas his conscience told him that the single-minded pursuit of God was the only worth-while occupation.

In order to try to reconcile this dilemma, he went to Holstein to live with Bourignon for a period, but she herself was under the threat of expulsion, due to her religious activities. Such a volcanic atmosphere was the last thing he needed, and he felt obliged to leave.

Returning to Amsterdam, Swammerdam turned to his old friend, Steno, who by this time had become a Catholic bishop. Steno found a patron who was willing to make him a payment of 12,000 guilders, and provide him with everything necessary both for his personal comfort and the continuance of his work. Swammerdam consulted Bourignon as to whether he should accept this offer, but following her advice, rejected it out of hand.

By now, his aging father had lost all patience and reduced his allowance by half. In desperation, Swammerdam tried to dispose of his collection of specimens, but could find no buyers. He decided to retire and shun all earthly interests. When his father died, the museum was sold, but realised only a fraction of its true value. Swammerdam's sister received a large proportion of the estate, leaving him almost destitute. He became sick with dropsy, and completely melancholic. After making a will leaving everything to Thevionot, Swammerdam died a broken man in 1680.

A few years before his death, Swammerdam had sent some papers to the Royal Society in London in order to achieve some recognition. but after his death most of his unpublished work almost went astray. Fortunately, after many upheavals, a man named Herman Boerhaave gathered all his letters and papers together, and it was he who was responsible for the publication of **The Book of nature** in 1737.

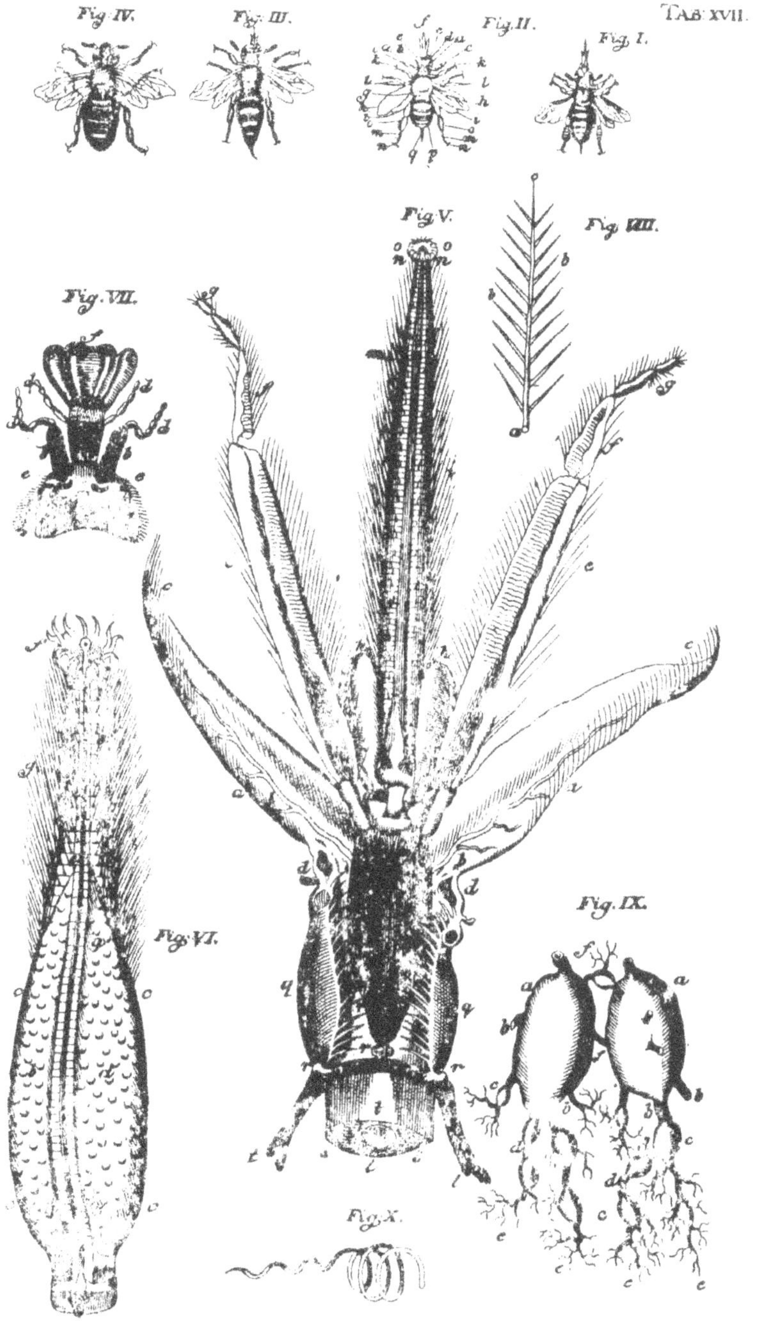

Drawings from "Book of Nature"

By the time he was thirty-six, Jan Swammerdam had become a pioneer of microscopy. He had also been the first to describe red corpuscles of the blood, the sporangia of the fern, and valves of lymphatic vessels. That these achievements, together with the detailed studies of insects, and more, could have been accomplished under these circumstances, in so short a life, is almost beyond credibility. To his father, himself by no means a nonentity, Swammerdam remained a bitter disappointment, a son who forsook a remunerative profession to follow his own obscure devices. As to Swammerdam himself, in the last seven years of his life, spent in sickness and poverty, the rich harvest of his fertile talents can have seemed little more than a futile waste.

Now, three hundred years after his death, there seems to be more in Swammerdam's life than a mere catalogue of achievement. To simple beekeepers as they go about their business, and scientists as they probe yet further along the trails he started, there must be some sense of humility that one man can have accomplished so much. Perhaps, too, the spirit of Swammerdam may evoke some contemplation on the profundities of life which we are no nearer to resolving than he was .

Chapter Four

THE 18th CENTURY

From: "The General Apiarian" by Jacob Isaac (1799).

From the fresh awakening of interest during the seventeenth century, due in no small measure to the impetus of Charles Butler's great work and the bee-minded members of the Royal Society, one might perhaps expect to find great advances being made in beekeeping in the years which followed. But this was not so. There was progress in the sense that greater efforts were made to replace conjecture with hard scientific fact, but it often took many, many years for such facts to be put to practical use in the apiary.

Much of this scientific work took place on the continent, and it was sometimes years before its results were available elsewhere, as was the case with Swammerdam. At the end of the seventeenth century the Royal Society had published the work of the Italian physiologist, Malpighi, who had discovered the thread-like Malpighian tubes which are located in the upper abdomen of the bee, and act in a similar way to kidneys in mammals, but it was not until 1742 that Maraldi's **Observations sur les Abeilles** (1712) was translated into English. Maraldi, incidentally, was also Italian, and he added substantially to the knowledge of the physiology of the bee. The work of Reaumur, a much used source for later writers, was adapted and simplified by G. A. Bazin, and published in London in 1744. Reaumur is remembered for establishing beyond doubt the function of the queen in the life cycle of the colony. He utilised his skills as a physicist in an exhaustive study of bees, including temperature regulation in the hive.

As the inventor of the Reaumur thermometric scale, this interest in temperature in relation to bees is hardly surprising, although it represents but a tiny part of his amazingly wide scientific interests. Mention should also be made of the German, Schirach, who discovered in 1761 that queens can be raised from worker eggs.

R. A. F. de Reaumur

In the meantime, the British scientists were by no means asleep. Arthur Dobbs published a paper in 1750 describing how pollen was collected from one species of a plant at a time, and the function of the queen's sperinatheca. A few years later a surgeon, John Hunter, corrected Dobbs' theory that wax emanated from the bee's faeces, and also established that swarming bees were replete with honey. In addition, Hunter noted that there was some significance in the dancing of bees, thereby anticipating the twentieth century work of von Frisch and Lindauer. In 1776 John Debraw, who was familiar with the work of Schirach, read a paper to the Royal Society in which he drew attention to the absorption of royal jelly underneath the egg. His theory regarding the fertilization of eggs was much respected at the time but, as we shall see in due course, evidence would soon be published which would end the need for speculative answers to this question.

So much, briefly, for the work of the scientists during this period, but what of The Practical Beekeepers? Evidence suggests that quite often the apiary was largely the province of the womenfolk, along with butter-making, attending to the poultry and so on. The frontispiece of Nathaniel Bailey's **Dictionarium**

Domesticum (1736) certainly suggests this, and although the lady illustrated was not shown as being actively engaged with the bees, other contemporary writers confirm the point. Furthermore, a Devonshire lady, Mrs. Sarah Harrison, wrote some pages about beekeeping in **The Housekeeper's Pocket Book** (1733).

It was a book by Joseph Warder, however, which had the greatest influence on beekeepers during the first half of the eighteenth century. Warder was a

physician who lived in Croydon, and perhaps the note made by a previous owner of Col. H. J. O. Walker's copy of the book provides an interesting thumb-nail sketch. of this man: "The author of this tract has been a Presbyterian, a Soldier, a Quack, and everything. But for bees, I have been aquainted by some Gentlemen who have had ye curiosity to visit his Bee-hives, that no man in ye world did probably understand them better." This book is now in the Miller Library, Madison, U.S.A., which bought Col. Walker's collection in 1929. (Col. H. J. O. Walker was a beekeeper who lived at Budleigh Salterton, in Devon, an authority on the history of beekeeping. He catalogued the books in the B.B.K.A. library in 1912, and the catalogue of his own collection is recognised as an important bibliographical tool).

First published in 1712, Dr. Warder's **The True Amazons** was very well received, and the book ran to nine editions, the last appearing in 1765. Queen Anne graciously accepted the dedication of the second edition, and this no doubt enhanced the author's prestige. Naturally, Warder received criticism of his work, and it is just possible that the claim that his book was a "new discovery and improvement" invited such criticism. In fact, it is an honest and remarkably well ordered description of Bees and Beekeeping by an obviously capable beekeeper, but there is frankly not very much by way of discovery or improvement about it. Warder was undoubtedly an observant beekeeper, and he performed a few experiments, or occular demonstrations as he nicely calls them, to show that bees stayed by the queen, but these were nothing like the intensive and systematic experiments which later were shown to be necessary by others.

Warder himself was critical of Moses Rusden, and the reader may find the language interesting. It concerns bees' reproduction. "I confess it was a bold stroke of Mr. Rusden, to lay down such a hypothesis. and impose it on the world as a matter of fact without giving us one rational argument to prove it, or anyone experiment by which he was let into the secret." Warder then goes on to give a description of the reproductive organs of the drone in such colourful details as can seldom have been equalled. He was, of course, not much closer to the truth than Moses Rusden, for Warder believed that the workers, not the "King bee," were responsible for laying the eggs!

Warder is also at some pains to correct "the good woman of the house to whose protection for the most part the bees are committed." What was the point in destroying a strong two-year old stock, because the bees will all be too old for the following season? Warder well appreciates the woman's temptation of "a good lump of honey, and a firkin of good mead fit to be tapped at Christmas," but points out that the bees "taken by storm in the night ... and slain by fire," will by no means be old and worn-out.

It is interesting to read Warder's directions and opinions about the ways and means of beekeeping, and the writing is often pleasingly conversational, but quite often the homilies delivered as asides are even more arresting.

For example, Warder is strongly moved by what he calls the loyalty of the queen, and in the course of his rather lengthy description, we are suddenly reminded of the political conditions of The Times.

"Oh; that all the thousands of this Britanic-Israel were but so loyal to our most gracious King George, who by all the sacred ties of law and nature, hath an undoubted right to, and by his boundless clemency and goodness, doth in the highest manner deserve our utmost loyalty. Where Britons, where is your boasted loyalty, that the very insects of your country shall reprove you? Whilst they join their forces together with an undivided fidelity, against all that dare presume to invade either the crown, or territories of their queen? You degenerate too often into faction, the very seeds of rebellion, which hath hurried you blindly on, even once to the dipping of your sacrilegious hands in the blood of your sovereign. But to stay no longer on the melancholy degression, in hopes the fidelity, courage and loyalty of my bees may teach you your duty."

Not all Warder's strictures are couched in such forbidding tones, and he is usually more gentle. In one chapter he gives directions to the carpenter how to make a bee-house for six colonies. They are such a model of clarity and precision that almost anyone could follow them. Again, he writes a charming little chapter on how to bring dead bees alive by putting them in the breeder's trouser pocket,-"the coat or the waistcoat not being warm enough,"-or by holding them in his hand,-twenty or thirty at a time.

Imported wines were becoming popular at this time, and Warder gives directions for the making of mead, "In no way inferior to the best of Spanish wines ... It is best kept till it is a year old; and if you make it well will keep as long as you please. I have some now by me almost nine years old."

So, Joseph Warder with his plain and easy directions showed how to manage bees in straw hives, or transparent boxes. If the summers were kind, an outlay of four or five pounds would get you thirty or forty pounds per annum. It is not surprising that the good doctor of Croydon did well with his book. Among

Warder's critics, mentioned earlier, there are two which are interesting. The first Irish bee book, **Instructions for Managing Bees**, published by the order of the Dublin Society in 1733, expressed disapproval of the bee boxes he described, and preferred straw hives kept in a bee house. Another critic was the Reverend John Thorley who visited Warder, although the doctor was away at the time. Having ridden out from London, Thorley was determined to see this profitable system of management for himself, and he persuaded the doctor's son-in-law to take him to the house. What he saw certainly did not please him. He found the boxes painted with lions and other creatures, which he thought was quite shocking. The colonies were also weak, and not sited as well as they might have been. As to the fifty pounds a year income which Warder claimed, Thorley thought the annual profits of such an apiary would certainly be less than ten pounds. At night, he returned to the City, greatly disappointed not to have learned anything new, and saddened that people had given him the wrong impression. Thorley probably kept a still tongue, however, because he was given some of the doctor's mead, and this he proclaimed to be very good.

Joseph Warder

Thorley himself lived at Chipping Norton, in Oxfordshire, and he was not unlike Warder in some respects. He promised his readers a new, easy and effectual method of "preserving bees," based on forty years' experience. He may have read Warder's book during his early days as a beekeeper - certainly, he was familiar with it, also with Gedde and Rusden. Rather curiously, the Reverend Charles Butler is always referred to as Doctor Butler, an error of which later writers have sometimes been guilty. The book by Daniel de Foe's son-in-law, Henry Baker **Microscope made Easy** had been published only a couple of years before Thorley's **Melisselogia** (1744), but Thorley had read it.

The frontispiece to **Melisselogia** is interesting because it is a copy by T. Loveday of Cesi's three bees, which was the first drawing of bees made with the help of a microscope in 1625. It was reprinted by Northern Bee Books in 1977. Loveday was responsible for three other illustrations in the book, one of which shows the writer seated at his study desk, by an open window, and has since been reproduced several times. .

Dr. A. Malcolm Fraser describes him as an old man, and whilst the evidence suggests that Thorley was probably well into middle age when he wrote this book, the illustration seems to this writer to be of a younger man. The face shows a noble forehead, somewhat sensuous lips and well-spaced eyes. His right hand is using a pen, whilst his left is sifting amongst a number of bees which are lying stupefied on the table. More will be said about this in a moment, but in the meantime, it is interesting to note that outside the window a swarm is settling in a tree, under which stands half a dozen straw hives, in a row on a bench. This may have been a liberty taken by the illustrator, because Thorley favours the octagonal hive, and elsewhere there is a drawing which seems to have been copied from Rusden's book. But, to return to the bees on the table; these were the result of "a secret unknown to past ages, and now published for the benefit of mankind. "

Rev. John Thorley

What then was Thorley's great discovery? In a word, it was the puffball, which has a narcotic effect on bees when used as smoke. Now, there is no more pious book on beekeeping than the Rev. John Thorley's **Melisselogia** yet the question must be asked - what made him decide to take a giant puffball, wrap it. in paper and, after the household bread had been baked, put it into the' oven overnight to dry? And, having ignited a piece about the size of a hen's egg, fix it on to a pointed stick and use the smoke to stupify his bees?

These puffballs had many names - bunt, puckfist, frogcheese, pucks, -and the truth is that their characteristics had been known by country folk for ages. John Gerard's **The Herball** (1597) says: "In some places of England they use (them) to kill or smolder their bees," and goes on to say how they were used to carry fire from place to place. The dried fungus was also used by surgeons to stop bleeding.

Had John Thorley not said that the secret was "unknown to past ages," and that he was "the first to inform his readers" and so on, the matter might pass unnoticed. Was he ignorant about the use of puffballs, or did enthusiasm run away with his pen? The reader might conclude that Thorley's claim was related merely to the uniting of stocks, and not to the properties of the puffball.

Whatever the answer, the overwhelming impression given by **Melisselogia** is one of piety, and one sometimes wonders about the length and severity of Thorley's sermons in church. "And as perfect justice reigns among them at home, so are they likewise honest in their labours abroad, gathering nothing but what is their own, and the Great Lord of All allows them. "

Thorley was a sound beekeeper, and a careful observer. His stupifying technique enabled him to weigh and count a swarm, and so arrive at one of the first estimates of the weight of a bee. He saw wax on a bee's abdomen, and thereby cleared up the question of the origin of this substance, a problem which had baffled earlier writers. He also saw a queen lay eggs as she ran across his hand, and so ended the long dispute as to whether this bee was male or female. On the other hand, he was convinced that copulation played no part in breeding, and that workers were neither male nor female.

The story about a swarm settling on Thorley's servant girl, and how by finding and removing the queen he prevented her from the slightest harm has been re-told by several writers. It is one of several anecdotes which add to the warmth and humanity which is characteristic of the best writers on beekeeping.

At one time Thorley was Chaplain to the Lord Mayor of London, and this may help to account for the long list of subscribers to his book. These included the Governor of the Bank of England, knights, lawyers and clergymen. It may also have been due to the fact that his son, N. Thorley, had premises in Lombard Street, from which he sold a hive of his own invention. The son was also the selling agent for **Melisselogia** and the address given on the title page is the Lock and Key, facing the Mansion House. Subsequent editions of the book were published by N. Tholey, and and it is interesting to note that pirate editions, omitting the theological references, were published in 1745 and 1760. These pirate editions also included matter from Bazin's **The Natural History of Bees** (1744).

Like almost every other writer, Thorley felt very strongly about the destruction of colonies as a means of taking the honey. He was, like Warder, a professional man, and their interest in bees was essentially that of the amateur. An altogether different character followed them into the limelight in 1768, when Thomas Wildman published a treatise on the management of bees. Wildman was more in the mould of John Gedde. He was an extrovert with an eye for the main chance. Bees to him were meat and drink, and his approach was generally brisk and businesslike. Not for him the moralising of John Thorley, or the amateurish discoveries of Rusden and Warder. Wildman was the confident bee-man, fully practised in his craft, who was bursting to sell beekeeping and willing to use the ballyhoo of a market trader.

These characteristics led Dr. Fraser to describe him as a charlatan, but there was more to Wildman than this. Undoubtedly, he was a showman, probably the most spectacular that beekeeping has ever seen, and although this may be a doubtful attribute in an essentially quiet occupation, it should not be allowed to detract from his genuine and serious approach to Bees and Beekeeping. Then again, perhaps there is an element of the showman in many beekeepers. How many of them have not been warmed by the approbation of curious on-lookers when they have successfully captured a swarm in some public place?

The difference in Wildman's case was that he gave circus-like performances with bees, well advertised and with a charge for admission. The practical difficulties of mounting such displays were undoubtedly considerable, but the underlying principles upon which he relied were quite simple. Basically, most of the spectators were afraid of bees, and the prospect of a man, without protection, handling a swarm of stinging insects was something akin to entering the lion's cage. Having built up this atmosphere of apprehension, Wildman would then persuade the bees to settle anywhere he wished by the simple expedient of controlling the queen on a silken thread. The climax of his performance was to stand on the back of a galloping horse, wearing a beard of bees!

Wildman's skill in manipulating. bees was well known, and John Mills, a contemporary writer, described two demonstrations which bear a close resemblance to the remarkable proceedings described above, although Wildman is not actually mentioned by name.

Incidentally, John Mills was a fellow of the Royal Society, and his **Essay on the Management of Bees** (1766), is interesting because it contains a summary of the work of Madame Vicat, as well as references to de Rearimr and other continental authorities. Madam Vicat was the aristocratic Swiss wife of an academic. Her papers were published by the Berne Society, and she was almost certainly the first women to show a scientific interest in bees. Her work was not translated into English, and it was to John Mills that Wildman was indebted for his knowledge of this and other material written in foreign languages. Unlike Mills, whose book is essentially a digest of other peoples' ideas, Wildman is both original and constructive. He was not a scientist, but as the inclusion of some natural history of the honeybee is necessary in relation to beekeeping, he provides a very readable account of this, based on the work of de Reamur and Maraldi. (Giacomo Maraldi was an Italian astronomer, who published a paper, **Observations sur les Abeilles** in 1712).

Scientist or not, however, Thomas Wildman's **Treatise on Bees** also provides an excellent essay on the subject of wasps and hornets, as perhaps the following short extract will indicate.

> "The bees are a pacific people that labour for our good, and in return we interest ourselves for them; other insects make war upon them, and consequently excite our enmity and abhorrence: they have no enemies more dreaded than the wasp, who are not content with plundering them, but likewise devour them. The wasps, compared with the mild and well-policed republic of bees, appear to us a savage nation, a kind of hottentots; but we judge thus ill of then only for the want of knowing them. We may apply to wasps, what hath often been observed with respect to a distant people, who have been thought barbarians, and are afterwards found to exceed us in many things. The republic of wasps are in nothing inferior to those of bees; although more warlike, they are not less industrious nor less laborious. In short, they are with respect to bees, what the ancient Spartans were with respect to the Athenians."

Wildman was meticulous in citing the sources he used, and one of these was a man named Richard Bradley. Now, Bradley was certainly no authority on bees, any more than he had first-hand knowledge of any of the incredibly wide range of rural subjects about which he published books. In fact, he wrote so many books during the first thirty years of the eighteenth century that even,

G. E. Fussell, **Old English Farming Books** (1523-1793), was uncertain that his list was complete. At a time when education was measured by a knowledge of classical languages, Bradley was totally deficient in this respect, and yet he managed to talk himself into the chair of Botany at Cambridge, promising amongst other things to found a public botanic gardens at the university. As for his remarkable output of books, many of them seem to have been written by others and issued under Bradley's name. Nevertheless, he was undoubtedly a man of considerable talent and achievement. In the matter of self-promotion and advancement, however, he could certainly have shown Wildman a clean pair of heels. Perhaps, had Wildman realised this, he might have learned more from Bradley than the usefulness of broom as a nectar source for bees, a fact which may have been culled from a translation of Pliny! Such fruitless conjecture, however, is to detract from both Wildman and Bradley, for their energy and enthusiasm alone would put most men to shame.

But what of Wildman the beekeeper? He was certainly highly proficient; he had worked out his own methods and designed his own hives. By no means bombastic, he invited comparison of his own hives with Madame Vicat's and the Rev. Stephen White's collateral bee boxes, suggesting that the reader himself decided which were best.

Wildman aimed at becoming something more than a capable beekeeper. His exhibitions were probably intended to encourage the better-off sections of the community to become interested in beekeeping, using Wildman's hives, of course, and also as a means of entertainment. The apiary should be sited "near the mansion-house, on account of the convenience of watching them." His intentions are made quite clear ... "to gentlemen who have leisure and genius, the objects on which their enquiries should be founded . . . these researches will be greatly forwarded by the ease with which the bees may be come at, both on the construction of my boxes, and of the command which my experience may now give every person over bees."

Quite clearly, Wildman was no fool! He was one of the first people to undertake to manage other peoples' bees for a fee, and with a living to earn, who could blame him for trying to make beekeeping attractive to the monied classes? In fact, he died whilst attending to bees at the house of one of his patrons. Wildman's book was translated into German and Italian, and his exploits were widely reported in the press. This Plymouth man, who had come to London in 1766, certainly made more of an impression on the general public than many beemasters. Indeed, when the first edition of **Encyclopedia Britannica** was published in Edinburgh, in weekly parts between 1768 and 1771, it contained long extracts from the pen of Thomas Wildman. In fact, "Wildman on Bees" appears in the list of authors, and he is certainly the principal contributor on the subject.

Also living in London about this time was Wildman's nephew, Daniel Wildman. On the face of it, the two men may have helped each other, but there seems to be no evidence that this was so. Daniel gave similar exhibitions with live bees, and on one occasion before King George III. These exhibitions took place nightly at the Jubilee Gardens, Islington, from 20th June, 1772. Seats cost 2/- (10p) and 1/- (5p). Daniel Wildman also gave exhibitions on the continent, and in 1773, he published a very successful book on beekeeping, which ran to many editions. The book was translated into French, and in 1792 a farmer, of Massachusetts, used substantial parts of it in one of the earliest American bee books.

Daniel Wildman also had a fair eye for business, and he opened a shop in Holborn for selling his own hives, honey and so on. He was probably the first appliance dealer in beekeeping. He also kept hives of thriving bees on the roof of his house in Holborn.

Of the two Wildmans, Thomas is generally regarded the more highly, and his bee book is certainly one of the best produced in this field during the eighteenth century. It was reprinted in facsimile a few years ago, and has interested beekeepers over many generations. Interestingly, in **The Hive and the Honeybee** revised and re-written by C.P. Dadant (22nd Edition 1923), there are four quotations from Wildman, all with a practical relevance.

In the latter half of this century, there was an appreciable growth of interest in natural history. Gilbert White's **Natural History of Selborne** appeared in the eighties, and Oliver Goldsmith's **History of the Earth and Animated Nature** a few years earlier. Neither of these popular works had any direct influence over the course of beekeeping, nor did the flamboyance of the Wildmans' totally eclipse other writers on bees. The names of John Keys and James Bonner come to mind. Both were practical beekeepers of long experience and as one might expect, did not always see eye to eye. Keys lived at Bee Hall, near Pembroke, whilst Bonner was from Auchencrow, near Berwick-on-Tweed, and it seems doubtful if the two ever met.

As luck would have it, Bonner's **A New Plan for Speedily Increasing the Number of Bee Hives in Scotland** appeared in 1795, just at the time when Keys had completed **The Antient Bee-Master's Farewell**. Keys adds a critical postscript to his work, unable to accept, as Bonner had done, Schirach's "doctrine of raising young queen bees at pleasure, in order to form artificial swarms" - i.e. the raising of queens from worker larvae. On the other hand, Keys was very quick to demolish Bonner's incredible plan for increasing the number of beehives. This was to start with five stocks *"which the second year* *will be increased to ten, and so continue to increase in a duplicate ratio for ten years, which will then amount to 2,560. . • . I sincerley hope, as Mr. B. has been a practitioner for twenty-six years, he has accumulated a snug fortune to compensate for his labours and ingenious discoveries".*

Bonner, however, was by no means without ability. His father, another James Bonner, had tutored his son well in the pleasures and profits of beekeeping, with the result that the young man soon graduated from watching his father's bees at swarming time to the management of hives of his own.

Bonner senior reckoned that in good seasons the bees would provide sufficient to pay for oatmeal to feed his large family for the year, and one foot note. year he was able to purchase a large quarto bible from selling the wax. In addition, the house was always well supplied with honey, and a kind of weak mead which was drunk all the year round. A weaver by trade, he also had an exceptionally retentive memory and could repeat whole passages from scripture verbatim. He worked right up to the time of his death at the age of eighty-six.

James Bonner, the youngest of twelve children, was every bit as enthusiastic as his father, and not only did he read all the bee books available, and carry out all manner of experiments with bees, he also made a special journey from Berwickshire to London to converse with Mr. Wildman. Unfortunately, Wildman -probably Daniel- was away in France at the time, so he contented himself with buying all the available books on the subject before making what was in those days the long and hazardous journey back home.

In **More Old English Farming Books** (1950), G. E. Fussell writes: "Bonner emphasizes the uses of bees and the chiefá obstacles to beekeeping in Scotland, not only the bad weather, but the negligence of the wealthy and the inability of the poor to buy more hives or to invest their little at the risk of failure, though there were plenty of flowers, white clover and, on the wastes, heather, furze and broom."

James Bonner seems to have built-up a good market for honey for he supplied the nobility and gentry in Edinburgh, Newcastle and elsewhere. He tells how he was carrying "a few very fine honey combs, to a gentleman in the New Town," when he met the President of the Board of Agriculture, Sir John Sinclair, a man whose influence Bonner had coveted for some time. Any diffidence which Bonner had previously felt was quickly dispelled by this casual meeting, and Sir John soon became influenced by Bonner's enthusiasm. His plans for developing beekeeping were put by Sir John to the Highland Society, and with their seal of approval, Bonner was not long in organising a subscription list which, as he said, "Far exceeded his most sanguine expectations." The list is included in **A New Plan**... and includes merchants, medical men, lawyers, titled people, not to mention an innkeeper, a joiner and a teacher of dancing.

The publicity was certainly brilliant, but it seems doubtful if the long-term course of beekeeping was changed at all by this burst of interest. Bonner, like Wildman, offered his services to any gentlemen, or lady, with regard to the management of bees in any respect, although he does not mention the fee.

Finally, mention should be made of William White, of Shutford, near Banbury. He wrote a delightful little book, **A Complete Guide to the Mystery and Management of Bees** (1771). White apologises for his "not having had the advantage of a grammatical education," ... but ... "I flatter myself there is not one in Europe better qualified to judge of the management proper for those useful insects than myself, having for thirty years made them my constant study, and by experiments, attained the certainty and infallibility of the methods I have prescribed."

Such apparent bombast runs intermittently through the whole of beekeeping literature, right up to the present day. It is usually deceptive for, like William White, most of these - "cottage writers" (it is the only term which springs to mind) - care so deeply for their subject that they feel compelled almost against their better judgement, to put their pens to paper. White was one of the first of these salt-of-the-earth beekeepers, and far from being a braggart, a closer association reveals him to be a kindly companion.

Important though the patient observations of practical beekeepers have been throughout the years, many beekeeping problems would have not have been solved without the aid of the scientists. In the next chapter, we shall consider the life and work of a man who, despite a lack of formal training, had a natural gift for experiment and research; a unique and remarkable man.

Thomas Wildman

Chapter Five

Huber

The Huber Bracelet. From: Beeton's "Book of Poultry and Domestic Animals" (1870).

Francis Huber had what has been described as "a sufficiently capacious and impartial mind" required of a first-class scientist. Huber spent most of his life studying the honeybee; he made some important discoveries, but it is not enough to fit these discoveries into the jig-saw of progress; there are certain facets of his remarkable life which are worthy of particular consideration.

What is so exciting about Huber is not so much the progress he made, but the way he approached his work. He set new standards in thoroughness and method, and it is these which have continued to inspire his successors quite as much as the results he achieved. Nowadays, Huber commands universal respect and affection but, as we shall see later, even the truth is sometimes ridiculed.

Francis Huber, a Swiss, was born into a wealthy family. His father was a friend of Voltaire, and a man of artistic tastes, a capable musician and a minor poet. As a boy, Huber was influenced by these urbane and talented surroundings, and he read avidly. His future seemed destined to follow that of his father towards the arts and gracious living.

As so often happens in life, and indeed in beekeeping, events took an unexpected turn. At the age of fifteen, it became apparent that his eyesight was failing. His father took him to a specialist in Paris, who advised that the boy should lead a quiet life in rural surroundings.

From: Beeton's "Book of Poultry and Domestic Animals" (1870)

Country life was no hardship to Huber, and he took an interest in all the activities of the countryside; he learned to plough, observed the changing seasons and the effects they had on wildlife. As he matured, natural history took up more and more of his time, and eventually his attention became focussed on the honeybee. In the meantime, whilst his general health had improved, his eyesight continued to deteriorate.

At the age of eighteen, at a dancing class, Huber met the girl who was to become his wife, the daughter of a Swiss magistrate. As tiine went on, they wanted to marry, but the girl's father put every obstacle in the way to prevent his daughter becoming tied to a disabled man, restricted to a rural life. In the end, after seven years, the diminutive Maria was led to the altar by an uncle, and thus began a long and happy married life.

Later, when Huber became totally blind, he said of Maria, " ... as long as she lived, I was not sensible of the misfortune of being blind. " It was a typically generous remark of this amiable and contented man, who was entirely devoid of bitterness. Maria not only compensated for his lack of sight, she took a close interest in the things that interested Huber. He was by no means totally infatuated with bees. He could discourse on many subjects, and Huber's household gives the impression that it was both lively and good humoured.

The Hubers had a servant names Francis Burnens, and he was encouraged to help with the bees. Burnens had had very little formal education, but there is no doubt that he played a major part in Huber's early work. In the beginning, Burnens had simply been involved in reading aloud to Huber, particularly books on physics and natural history, but he became so interested that he was soon able to discuss these subjects on more or less equal terms with Huber. Realising that Burnens had a natural gift for scientific observation and experiment, Huber developed complete confidence in him, and the two men grew in stature together.

Class conscious writers in later periods have sometimes appeared to stress the servant relationship between Burnens and Huber, whereas in truth it was a remarkable partnership.

Burnens had great patience, and would sometimes work for twenty-four hours at a stretch without food or rest. Occasionally, he would be severely stung. "I often upbraid myself," Huber wrote, "For putting his courage andpatience to so hard a test, but he was as interested as I in the success of our experiments, and through the extreme desire which he had to become informed of the results, he counted as nothing the trouble, the fatigue and the temporary pains of the stings. Therefore, if there is any merit in our discoveries, I must divide the honour with him; it is a great satisfactionfor me to insure this reward for him, by acknowledging the justice of it publicly."

These words, of course, tell us as much about the character of Huber, as they do of Burnens. Huber had the creative mind which inspired their work, but what had influenced Huber himself? What had determined the nature of his experiments, and the clear-headed way in which they were conducted?

Briefly, there appears to be three direct sources for his inspiration, apart from a natural inclination towards this subject and a wide reading of scientific writers. First was the work of Swammerdam, second was an admiration of de Reaumur's experimental work, and third there was the catalyst which probably motivated as much as anything the course of the experiments: a naturalist and philosopher named Charles Bonnet.

Bonnet, like Huber, was born in Geneva (1720). He was thirty years older than Huber,and in 1745 had published a treatise on insects. He was a member of the Royal Society in London, and also a member of the Academy of Science, in Paris. Huber was friendly with Bonniet, and it was to Bonnet that the letters from the little village of Pregny, near Paris, were directed. These letters formed the basis of Huber's book. Incidentally, Bonnet, too, had defective vision, although he was not totally blind.

Huber's **Nouvelles Observations** were first published in French, in 1792, and the first translation into English was made by John Dalyell, a lawyer, and published in Edinburgh in 1806. There are later editions in both languages, but probably the most useful is the American translation by C. P. Dadant, published in 1926. Not only were corrections made in this edition, but it also includes the original twelve plates, against only five in the Englishtranslation, as well as additional material which was omitted. In fact, the Dadant edition contains no less than ten further chapters prepared for publication by Huber's son, Pierre. The modern reader is fortunate to have this complete translation which was performed "as a labour of love" by one of the most eminent beemasters of his day.

Pierre Huber, by the way, became a distinguished naturalist in his own right. He seems to have had a marvellous relationship with his father, a circumstance which is not all that common when different generations of one family are engaged together in a narrow field. Pierre Huber later himself published an important treatise on ants, although his work on bees continued to be published in his father's name.

In a way, Francis Huber's disability may well have been contributory to the unity and happiness of his family life. As we have seen, both wife and son were able to participate in his activities, while Burnens, of course, was a pillar of strength until he eventually left the family to become a magistrate -doubtless as a result of the Huber family influence. Huber also had a daughter who looked after him after Maria's death, and it was in her arms that he died on 22nd December, 1831, in his eighty-first year.

On the subject of Huber's blindness, C. P. Dadant remarks:

"Milton is believed by many to have been a better poet in consequence of his blindness; and it is highly áprobable that Huber was a better apiarist from the same cause. His active, yet reflective mind demanded constant employment; and he found in the study of the honeybee full scope for his powers."

Huber is probably best remembered because he established beyond all doubt the manner whereby the queen is fertilised, a subject which had been for so long a matter of conjecture. As Dadant so rightly points out, Huber's work is an admirable specimen of the inductive system of reasoning, and the letters on this subject in particular are indeed a joy to read.

In 1951, however, this achievement was slightly tarnished. Dr. Fraser published a survey of the work of a Corinthian peasant named Jansha, who had found his way to the Vienna School of Art as an engraver at the age of thirty-two. Coming from a beekeeping family, he later obtained the job as a beekeeping instructor, and in 1770 he was appointed Imperial and Royal Beekeeper. He wrote a couple of books, and described quite accurately the fecundation of the queen. In other words, he appears to have been twenty years ahead of

The Hive of Huber

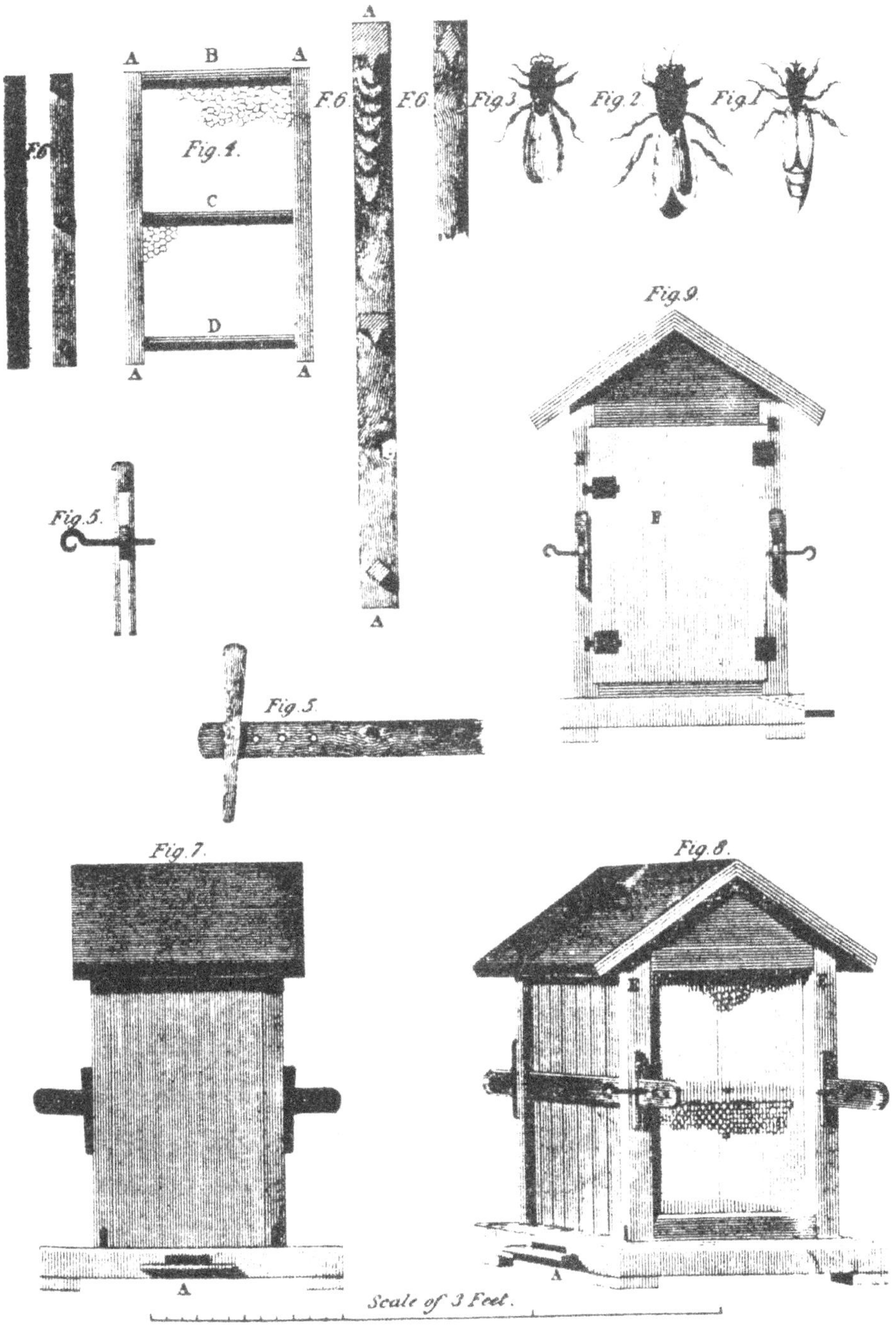

Huber. It may seem curious that Jansha's observations remained un-sung for so long, and indeed it may just be possible that others had suspected the truth, but had not published their theories. There was certainly no shortage of plausible explanations, but it was Huber that set up the experiments and proved the matter beyond doubt. Of course, his work did not end there, and he was able to clarify a number of problems.

One of the fundamental difficulties in bee research at that time was how to see what was happening within the darkness of the .hive. The existing glass walled hives were of little help, and Huber devised a set of frames on hinges which could be opened out like a book. The so-called "Leaf-hive" was certainly an influence on many designers of beehives for a considerable period, although it had no practical merit as it stood. Essentially, it was an observation hive, and served Huber well, but it bears little relation to modern observation hives.

Among other things, Huber noted that if the mating flight was delayed, or did not take place at all, the queen could still lay eggs. He was not able to explain that they would all hatch into drones. He was, however, able to clear up misunderstandings about propolis, wax and pollen; how they originated and how they were used. He also confirmed Schirach's theory of 1760 that workers could raise queens from worker larvae by feeding royal jelly, and thereby helped to settle the storms which had followed the publication of the German clergyman's statement.

Huber's own work was by no means universally acclaimed, as we shall see in the following chapter. On the other hand, he was not quite a prophet without honour in his own land. He was admitted to the Academy of Sciences of Paris, and he had many friends.

It is difficult to resist mentioning that whilst Huber was in his garden quietly strolling along paths marked by threads, with the smell of the summer flowers, "and the hum of bees working like incidental music to his contemplations, elsewhere in France, Napoleon was making history of another kind.

Or, again, that Huber's blindness, believed at the time to have been brought on by too much youthful study, had been caused by cataracts: a condition which is nowadays usually curable, even in elderly people.

Over the years, beekeepers and others have derived philosophical satisfaction from the lives and work of honeybees. The life and work of Francis Huber is another such source, capable of yielding more than the measurable facts. How much more may perhaps be a reflection of the depth of the onlooker's perception?

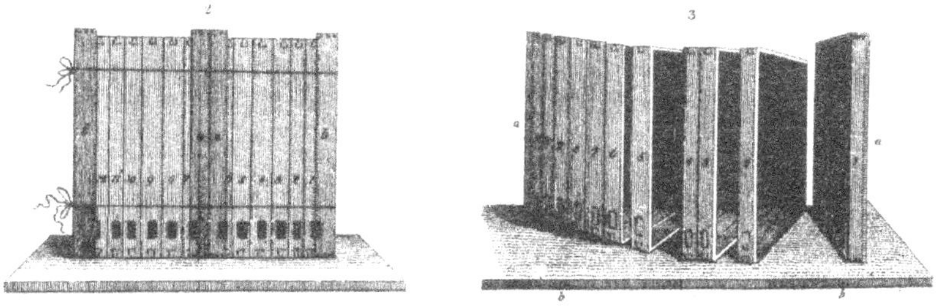

The Hive of Huber

Chapter Six

THE 19th CENTURY

From: "Scenes of Industry" (1827).

It was not until the latter half of the nineteenth centurythat development of modern methods of beekeepingbegan to gather momentum. The tide had changed with Huber, and there was a marked upsurge of interest in natural history as well as in practical beekeeping, but there were many false dawns. Men continued to publish books making over-confident promises about easy methods and new equipment. These inevitably failed to live up to expectations, and were in most cases too elaborate and costly for the average beekeeper. But if progress seemed hesitant, the signs of impending change became increasingly evident. Right from the seventeenth century the call to abandon the annual slaughter of thebees had been fruitlessly echoed by virtually everywriter on practical beekeeping. Despite this, the practice continued to be widespread until well into the twentieth century. As we shall see later, when the time was ripe, leaders emerged capable of organising and educating the beekeepers in a coherent manner, but thus far such efforts had not succeeded.

In 1801, for example, the Western Apiarian Society was formed in Exeter, but the organisation remained localised, and it faltered after nine years of useful activity. Another society, proposed by a beekeeper named Robert Huish, a few years later, was still-borne, although Huish was a man of strong character, and had considerable influence among the beekeepers of his day. "Excepting the Spanish," wrote Huish, "I know of no nation which entertains such superstitious prejudices, in regard to bees, as the English," and it was partly because of this that he had the idea of organising an apiarian society. There was, for instance, a widely held belief that a purchased hive never prospers, and Huish thought that if this notion could be overcome by means of example, with the cottagers learning from a society, the way to better beekeeping would be cleared. Unfortunately, the help promised from "a high quarter" was not forthcoming, and the plan was dropped. Perhaps Huish was too over-bearing for the beekeepers, and possibly his sponsor also.

Undoubtedly, he was well read in the literature of beekeeping, and appears to have been capable of translating both French and German. He had travelled widely, and always talked to other beekeepers whenever the opportunity arose. That he had a very good opinion of both himself and his abilities was plain enough. Had he not had twenty years of practical beekeeping experience with sixty to a hundred hives? Had he not talked to the Italians and the Germans, notto mention the French, read their findings, and for all these years had himself observed the activities of the bees? With these credentials, he regarded himself as a professional, well qualified to explain the mysteries surrounding the life ofthe honeybee and the best ways of managing an apiary.

Robert Huish

He was, of course, a contemporary of Huber, but where Huish's head was full of the theories of other people, and he was over-anxious to prove that surely he must have the right answers, Huber was much less dogmatic. Huber pieced his evidence together bit by bit, leaving nothing to conjecture, but Huish sometimes gives the impression that he was sorting things out as his pen raced along. His **Treatise on Bees** (1815) is full of crusading enthusiasm, and although his brash confidence is sometimes irritating, he certainly knew quite a lot about bees.

As a practical beekeeper, he found it hard to accept some of Huber's discoveries. He could agree, for example, that, "If too great a diameter be not given to the abode of the bees, it may without danger be increased in the elevation." He could agree that pollen was necessary for the nourishment of the young stock, but the idea of the queen being mated in the air merely showed how far an able naturalist, labouring under a defect of vision, would go in order to be the founder of a system. Further, "A smile will no doubt sit on the countenance of everyone in the least conversant with bees" at the idea that bees constructed wax fortifications against the moth. "The patent must be vested in the bees of Geneva," he concluded.

Huish also poured scorn on Huber's description of the way cells are constructed, and he was quite unable to accept his findings on the origin of wax, which according to Huish, was collected like pollen and water.

Naturally, many of the ideas put forward by Huish have little relevance to modern beekeeping, but his efforts in evaluating the conflicting opinions of the time, and his forthright style, appealed to many beekeepers. His scientific knowledge was rather weak, but he seems to have produced good crops of honey and, of course, he denounced the destruction of stocks as a means of gathering the honey crop.

Although Huish is sometimes described as a skeppist, it would be truer to say that he believed that straw, properly used, was the best material from which to build hives. He invented a type of hive which was shaped like a flower pot, and had moveable boards on which the combs hung.

In 1819, he published **Instructions for Using the Huish Hive**. (A facsimile edition of this pamphlet was published by Northern Bee Books, in 1980). Discussing the methods whereby a swarm could be persuaded to take to a new hive, Huish discounts the ideas that the hive should be rubbed with honey, syrup or bean leaves. "It may appear visionary to the incredulous apiarian, but I can mention a liquid which will induce bees to take to a hive sooner than all the honey and syrups which can be mentioned, and this is human urine; nor will this appear so improbable as many persons regard it, when it is considered that that liquid abounds in sugar and salt, two substances to which bees testify the greatest partiality. I strenuously recommend every person to sprinkle their hives with it, previously to putting the swarm into it, and they will be convinced of the specific virtue with which the liquid in question is endowed."

In a footnote, Huish describes how the Earl of C ... , accompanied by two of his sisters, called upon him to consult him about various beekeeping matters. One of the questions was about the hiving of swarms, and Huish mentioned that he knew of a liquid which "possessed the sovereign virtue or retaining bees in a hive." His Lordship pressed Huish strongly to disclose this secret, but the embarassed Huish felt unable to do so. When the party left, they were still in ignorance, and somewhat displeased; they could not understand why Huish, who had otherwise been so forthcoming, had failed to explain this simple point!

Robert Huish had started beekeeping in his late teens, and produced A **Treatise on Bees** by the age of forty. He has since been described as an obscure and unscrupulous scribbler, and before he died in 1850, at Camberwell, at the age of seventy-three, he had in fact written about crime and travel, as well as some moral tales. He had also written at least one poem **The Peruvians**. His reputation as a beekeeper was enhanced by the regular column on beekeeping which he wrote for a gardening magazine over a number of years.

He was a man of tremendous energy, and always ready to give advice, although he was often tactless and sometimes his advice was not well received. On one occasion, when walking through a Sussex village, he pointed out to some cottagers that their hives were much too close to the ground. But the cottagers were unmoved by this gratuitous advice and took no notice. Huish was not at all surprised because "the hives were in charge of the female part of the family," and consequently the could not be reached by reason! His opinion of women was never very high, and he suggests elswhere that the reason why stocks are sometimes bad-tempered is because they have a female at their head!

Whilst in Scotland, Huish visited James Bonner, whose reputation by this time had spread considerably. Huish, however, was not particularly impressed by Bonner's work, but one day when the two men were examining a hive together, the bald-headed Bonner received multiple stings on his head. Apparently, Huish was quite flabbergasted, because Bonner simply carried on as though nothing had happened, and the stings had no effect. Because Huish had not developed any immunity to stings himself, he could hardly credit that Bonner had done so. Needless to say, Huish had a remedy. "I know of no remedy more efficacious than treacle of Venice, or olive oil." As to Bonner, well, he was clearly something of an oddity! ("Treacle of Venice", by the way, was an electuary composed of many substances and used as an antidote to poison).

It is perhaps not surprising that Huish was given to exaggeration. For example, his catalogue of the enemies of bees is quite formidable and slightly misleading. Few would disagree with his broad conclusions, however. Next to man and the moth, Huish suggests that mice are the most troublesome. He provides a description of the traps which he set amongst his hives, although whether or not they were successful may best be judged from the description which follows:

> "Let a pea be soaked in water, then draw a thread through it and tying a small stick at each end, place them in the ground, the exact distance of the width of a brick; the brick is then placed on thread, and the mouse coming to eat the pea, gnaws also the thread, and the support being then taken away, it falls and kills the mouse."

Robert Huish, like William Herrod-Hempsall who was to playa dominant role in British beekeeping some hundred years later, came from Nottingham. In many ways, they were very much alike, especially in their enthusiasm and utter self-confidence. However, as we remarked earlier, the time for change was not yet ready, and whether Robert Huish could have played the part as effectively as Herrod-Hempsall, remains a matter for conjecture.

By means of his articles in the Gardner, (Florist and Apiculturist Huish) continued to interest beekeepers for many years in the practical aspects of the craft, but one of the most noteable changes during his lifetime was the growing interest in entomology. Many of these naturalists were clergymen such as the Rev. W. Kirby, whose **Monographia** (1802), listed more than three hundred species of native English bees. Kirby, in collaboration with William Spence, also produced the **Introduction to Entomology**. James Rennie, a professor of Zoology wrote several interesting books on insects as part of The **Library of Entertaining Knowledge** and in 1840, the Rev. W. Dunbar's **Natural History of Bees** was published in Jardine's **The Naturalists Library**.

The awakening interest was not confined to entomology. From Darwin's **Origin of Species** which appeared in 1859, and once described as the most important biological book ever written, there were numerous "popular" works, many designed for children. The Rev. J. G. Wood was a great popularizer, and his book on bees ran to several editions, including an American edition in 1863. There was a rising demand for books which provided "sound information a.nd innocent amusement: suited for all classes of readers," and natural history was a ready source for such entertainment and education.

My Bee Book by the Rev. W. C. Cotton was a work of this kind. It appeared in 1842, and was rather like a bed-side miscellany, or scrap book. Cotton's vicarage at Frodsham, in Cheshire,contained an enviable collection of bee books, later to be given to the Ministry of Agriculture, and it was largely from these that Cotton compiled his book. The book contains Cotton's letters to cottagers, which we shall consider shortly, and is a pleasant curio. Cotton is sometimes credited with the introduction of the honeybee into New Zealand, but an article in the **Cottage Gardner** 7th December, 1859, by "a Devonshire Beekeeper" (T. W. Woodbury), records that the bees were thrown overboard in bad weather. Whilst living in that country, he published a manual for beekeepers. He seems to have had squabbles with a couple of his British contemporaries. There was Thomas Nutt, for instance, the beekeeper who had started his working life as a draper's assistant, and whose work **Humanity to Honeybees** (1832), was remarkably successful for a number of years. Apparently, Cotton borrowed a plate from this book without permission, a matter to which Nutt referred in the sixth edition of his book. A couple of years earlier, in 1843, another beekeeper and appliance dealer, John Milton, had used some notes which Cotton had left with him in a book called **The Practical Beekeeper**. When Cotton returned from New Zealand, the two men had a row, and the notes were omitted in later editions.

William Charles Cotton was a mild eccentric, a typical amateur beekeeper of the upper middle classes which at the time were bringing their education and influence to bear on the craft. His interest in bees had been stimulated after his father, a governor of the Bank of England had read to him a translation of the fourth Georgic of Virgil. When the boy tried to obtain a bull calf so that the bloody process of obtaining bees from its carcass (as described by Virgil), could be tried out, a swarm was said to hav.e been quickly obtained from a neighbour. Be that as it may, Cotton's passion for bees remained with him for the rest of his life.

After attending Eton College, he went to Christ Church College, Oxford, and it was here that he founded the Oxford Apiarian Society. The rules of this Society, of which Cotton was the secretary and guiding light, were published in full in **My Bee Book**. The work of the Society, which did not flourish for long, impressed J. H. Payne, a beekeeper from Bury St. Edmunds, whose own first pamphlet **The Cottager's Guide**, (1832) had been published and distributed free of charge by the Suffolk and Norfolk Apiarian Society. Payne, incidentally, was the author of another small book **The Apiarian's Guide Containing Practical Directions for the Management of Bees upon the Depriving System**. This book ran to five editions between 1833 and 1851, each one slightly longer than its predecessor, and an indication of its usefulness.

Both Payne and Cotton were imbued with the idea of producing a short and simple guide for cottage beekeepers, and the societies with which they are associated are expresssions of this desire to help. In the case of Cotton, His **A Short and Simple Letter...** (1837) was said to have been written in one night whilst at Oxford. For a man who had gained a first-class honours degree in Classics, and a second in Mathematics (1836), it is repetitive and rather muddled. Not long after its publication a beekeeper of some twenty years experience, Richard Smith, wrote a lengthy criticism of Cotton's ideas in **The Cottager's Bee Book** (1839).

Cotton's interest in bees, however, remained undiminished. He travelled extensively in Europe for health reasons, being subject to mental illness. Amongst the results of his travels was the discovery of a book of comic verse by Wilhelm Busch, which he found whilst waiting for a train at Cologne Station, and which he freely translated into English as **Buzz a Buzz** (1872). On a more practical note, he was responsible for the first importation of carniolian Bees, in conjunction with Alfred Neighbour, a London appliance dealer.

Cotton's dream of a society for the advancement of beekeeping was realised before his death in an institution at Chiswick in 1879. He was a founder founder member of the British Beekeepers'Association, and was one of the judges at their first show at Crystal Palace in 1874. As a brother of Lord Justice Cotton, his impartiality was no doubt unquestioned!

Further references to the B.B.K.A., will be made in Chapter VII, but no doubt one day a full account of the history of this Association will be published to add and perhaps embellish the **B.B.K.A. Jubilee** (1928) by T. W. Cowan.

Returning now to John Milton, mentioned earlier, he was not the only appliance dealer to appreciate that the publication of a book sometimes helped to stimulate trade. Thomas Blow and Alfred Neighbour, both Quakers, incidentally, also published books. Another interesting character was T. W. Woodbury, who designed the first hive in Britain to incorporate the bee-space in a moveable frame hive, utilizing Langstroth's ideas. These ideas were thought to have been anticipated by another British beekeeper, W. A. Munn, in 1844, but speculation as to who originated various changes and modifications is inclined to be a complicated business. One thing is certain, there is seldom any shortage of new ideas in beekeeping, many of which turn out to be variations on old themes.

Neither is there any shortage of beekeepers ready and willing to put their ideas before the public, and along with the growth of literacy this became more noticeable as the nineteenth century progressed. One or two of these Victorian beemasters belong essentially to the twentieth century, and before closing this brief review of the nineteenth century, it seems right to look a little closer at two stalwarts of the old guard, so to speak.

In 1827, Dr. Edward Bevan published a lengthy book **The Honeybee, its Natural History and Management**. A second edition was dedicated to Queen Victoria. It is interesting because it is a comprehensive and authoritative statement of knowledge as it stood in early Victorian times. Bevan was a friend of W. A. Munn, who undertook a later revision of the book in 1870, but by the middle of the eiglities, F. R. Cheshire's two volume work had appeared and largely took its place. Cheshire was a schoolmaster, and although he seemed to go into print very shortly after taking up beekeeping, his major work on the scientific and practical aspects of the craft remained popular for some forty. years. Bevan, too, does not seem to have served an unduly long apprenticeship, and his study of bees served mainly to occupy an early retirement.

Bevan was a doctor of medicine who practised first at Mortlake and later at Congleton, in Cheshire. When ill health forced him to give up medicine, he went to live in Bridstow, Herefordshire, although he also appears to have lived at Llanferry, Carmarthen. In appearance, he has been described as being a chubby little man, remarkably like Mr. Pickwick.

Unlike Thomas Nutt, Bevan was not primarily a beekeeper, or an innovator, and simply kept half a dozen hives for observation and experiment. Bevan concenled himself with existing straw hives, bee boxes and bee houses, whereas Nutt was seeking to popularize the use of his collateral hives. Thomas Nutt's book "**Humanity to Honeybees**," (1832), is perhaps a good example of the over-enthusiastic selling of a 'fresh concept' in beekeeping, the new and easy fool-proof formula for success. Nutt said he had never read a book on the subject until his system had been published. The bees had been his instructors, he claimed. Edward Bevan, on the other hand, quotes from virtually every writer of any consequence, and although his book lacks the rather sensational 'discoveries' claimed by Nutt, it nevertheless continued to have an influence among beekeepers for some fifty years.

Dr. Bevan's introductory remarks are quite interesting. "Many of the tracts on bees are professedly written for the perusal of the cottager. To him, I do not so particularly address myself, as to the more intelligent members of the community; and so far as I am able to succeed in making an impression upon them, I shall consider myself as virtually benefitting the cottager. The latter is generally too much of a machine to be the first to adopt any improvement, however important; he is more likely therefore to obtain bee knowledge from the example or viva voce instruction of his enlightened neighbours than through the direct medium of the press. "

Although such an attitude may come as a shock to the modern reader, it simply reflects the social divisions of the time, and should not be regarded as providing any indications as to Bevan's character, or personality. Doctors in Victorian times came mainly from wealthy families, and general education for the lower orders still had to make its mark. His remarks simply reflect a class structure which was generally regarded as quite natural and proper.

Far from being a prig, Dr. Bevan proves himself to be a sympathetic listener, ready to lend an ear to any beekeepers willing to share their experiences with him. There was Mr. Golding from Maidstone, Mr. Humphrey from Staplehurst and Mr. Dewey from Melton Mowbray, for example, all of whom contributed to the process of testing the various theories under discussion. He was also in touch with the Rev. W. Dunbar and Dalyell, the translator of Huber. At every turn Bevan spares no effort, not only to take account of the ideas of contemporaries, but also to consider the work of naturalists and apiarians right from the ancient writers onwards.

But Bevan certainly did not simply cobble together a patchwork of other peoples' ideas. He was a careful observer himself, and indeed advises the pursuit of apiarian science as an antidote to boredom in retirement. His book is not one which a beginner could have easily turned to for immediate help; the available evidence is sifted over and the reader is left to make his own judgements.

After dealing at length with the physiology of the honeybee, Bevan goes on to tackle the subject which seems to form an obligatory chapter in most bee most bee books - the siting of the apiary! "The hives should not be exposed to the drippings of trees, nor be in the vicinity of noisome smells, nor disagreeable noises," and so on. Following lengthy discussion, he then mentions the celebrated Bonner, whose apiary was evidentally once situated in a garret in the centre of Glasgow!

Naturally, the best way to house the bees aroused some controversy, and from Bevan the modern reader can get a fair idea of the various alternatives which were then being considered. Thomas Nutt's collateral hives had aroused much enthusiasm. These "pavilions of nature" were boxes ten and a quarter inches cube, used side by side, with perforated tin tubes for ventilation. Bevan was not impressed with them, and cites numerous cases where they not only produced little or no honey, but swarmed as freely as any other.

"There has been some difference of opinion as to the most suitable dimensions of bee boxes," Bevan writes in the 1838 edition of **The Honey Bee**. "In the former edition of this work, a preference was given to those of Keys (see Chapter IV), but subsequent information and experience induce me to recommend their diameter to be three-eighths of an inch less than his, viz, eleven and five-eighths inches square by nine inches deep in the clear."

Edward Bevan

Rev. W. C. Cotton

Provision was made in these boxes for seven loose bars, and a door was fitted to give a view of the centre combs, as well as a glass window on each side. A thick top was secured with long tapered screws, and the floor was loose, extending one and a half inches beyond the back and sides, and with an outlet cut for the bees. A slide controlled the width of the entrance. These boxes could be used one on top of the other, and this was known as "storifying".

If the boxes were made out of lighter timber, a rough case made out of tea-chests could be placed over, and chaff or sawdust used for insulation. These suggestions seem to invite all sorts of trouble, but the double-walled principle was taken up by W. Broughton Carr some years later. The "W.B.C." hive was championed by Herrod-Hempsall, and it is Bevan whom he quotes when recommending Western Red Cedar as the best timber for hive construction.

Because comb is built downwards, boxes were often placed underneath the brood box, and this was known as "nadiring." As a general rule, Bevan suggested that old stocks should be supered (storified), ie. boxes placed above the brood box and that swarms should be nadired. Clean comb was kept from one season to another, and fixed to the bars as guide combs, and whilst the spacing of the brood comb needed to be accurate, combs used for honey storage could be given slightly more room to enable them to be extended. Although Bevan himself favoured the use of the wooden bee boxes, he recognised that straw skeps were used by the great majority of beekeepers, and he deals very thoroughly with this system, including methods whereby skeps could be storified and the destruction of the bees avoided.

These conditions favoured swarming, of course, and the beekeeper was advised to feed with sugared ale in February and March so that by swarming early, both parent stock and swarm might have a chance to produce a crop. Generally speaking, however, it was the second year stocks which gave the best results.

Bevan does not have a lot to say about robbing, but the remedy he borrowed from Schirach, the German beekeeper, does illustrate the confusion whioh was inevitable until more facts became available. The remedy was to unite a little wine or brandy with honey, and present it to the besieged stock. No explanation was given, and nothing is said about the results, if any, obtained. A drop of brandy was commonly used to ameliorate a human crisis, so perhaps it was judged that the bees would respond in the same way!

Bevan himself was convinced that bees had some power of reasoning, and he strongly disagrees with John Hunter, F.R.S. (author of an important paper read to the Royal Society in 1792), who was sarcastic about reason being attributed to insects. To illustrate the excursive fancy of apiarians, Hunter had, according to Bevan, selected an unfortunate example, namely that workers' eggs may be converted into queens!

To confuse matters further, Bevan later finds himself embroiled in a discussion as to the distinction between wisdom and knowledge. "The former alone can be possessed by the lower animals, man alone can possess both. "

> "Knowledge and wisdom, far from being one have oft times no connection. Knowledge dwells In heads replete with thoughts of otherness, Wisdom in minds attentive to their own". (Cowper)

"Insect reason is more restricted than the reason of man. The possession of organs of sense implies the possession of some portion of intellect, for without intellect those organs would seem incapable of being employed to the greatest advantage. "

Dr. Bevan, like other scientists of those days, was exercising intellect and reason to explain the activities of bees, but it was not by these means that answers were eventually found. It was to take years of research and observation by numerous people to provide the explanations, which even to-day are not complete.

Nevertheless, Bevan applied himself with great industry to delineate both the background and the current opinion about Bees and Beekeeping. He made no great discoveries, but he helped to pave the way for the advances which were soon to come.

Finally: let us turn from one doctor to another, further evidence of the middle-classes' deep involvement in Victorian beekeeping, but in this case his inclusion is not because of any technical merit. In fact, Dr. John Cumming could not honestly be described as a beemaster, although his work reflects remarkably clearly the way many beekeepers were thinking at the time. With Cumming's book, published in 1864, we are in a way looking at the end of an era in beekeeping, and sometimes it is difficult to believe that this is not a much older book than it is.

The book consists mainly of a series of anonymous letters written to **The Times** and it will come as no surprise to some that the author lived in Tunbridge Wells! These letters really offer little more than a few comments on amateur beekeeping, although the book itself contains a number of quotations from other well known works. The odd thing is that Dr. Cumming's innocent letters should have produced a response of such surprising acrimony.

Generally speaking, beekeepers are not notably quarrelsome by nature, yet time and time again one comes across the most bitter arguments on matters which are often little more than minor differences of opinion. In this case, the critical letters are not published, but Cumming complains savagely about their intemperate language. "Had this good gentleman eaten more honey and drunk less vinegar, he would have written a more affectionate letter. "

The good gentleman in question was, W. B. Tegetmeier, a founder member of the Royal Entomological Society, who wrote for **The Field** until the age of ninety, and about 1869 had published a booklet called **Bees, Hives and Honey**. Tegetmeier was also an authority on poultry, pigeons and pheasants; the painter Millais, illustrated some of his work, which is indicative of his standing amongst his contemporaries.

Apart from this row between Tegetmeier and Cummings, which spilled over into other newspapers and also involved T. W. Woodbury: "the mere copyist from Devon", there were other correspondents who addressed enquiries of a fairly superficial nature to **The Times Beemaster.** These came from intending beekeepers who were fairly well off, rather from those lower down the social scale, and it was these who Cumming believed would greatly benefit from keeping bees. Again, this is a recurrent theme of many writers over the years. As early as 1784, John Keys, for example was arguing that beekeeping was more profitable than other forms of husbandry. Why was it, then, that beekeeping failed to prosper as well as perhaps it should have done?

If we look briefly at **The Times Beemaster's** advice, it may provide some pointers.

Dr. Cumming regarded a bee-house as essential, and he describes several designs of sheds, "Made of good, strong, smooth deal and roofed with Croggon's patent roofing felt." Many of these bee-houses, or sheds, which were intended to protect the hives from the weather, were somewhat elaborate. They also tended to harbour all manner of unwanted insects.

As to hives, he favoured the Stewarton, which was stocked by neighbour Neighbour in his Regent Street shop, and imported from Scotland because the London craftsmen could not compete on the price. The Stewart on was a six-sided hive, and altogether too complicated for the average cottager to make himself, as Cumming suggested. He also rather liked Neighbour's straw hive which could be supered with a glass bell and had a woollen nightcap. Another hive was Pettitt's double box, which worked on a lateral principle with a zinc slide, and one of the arguments for this collateral system was that the bees suffered less fatigue than by climbing upwards in the storifying system!

Now, the truth is that none of these hives, and there were many others, really had very much to offer other than the prospect of a fairly small harvest of natural comb honey. They were all far more expensive, of course, than the simple straw skep which could be bought for less than a shilling at the time.

Dr. Cumming was quite well aware of this enormous disparity of costs, and he goes on to describe how a straw skep might be supered. One wonders how many of his readers tried, and were able to put the following instructions to good use.

In summary, the beekeeper was advised to wait until the honey flow, and at noon when most of the bees were out working, he was to cut an aperture about five inches in diameter with a sharp knife and then place either a bell-glass, or smaller skep over the hole. Then, as if to stiffen the resolve of the less confident, he goes on to enjoin - "If in cutting the hole on the top of the stock hive you lose your self possession, the watcher-bees will attack you. Decision invariably paralyzes them for the moment, and secures your safety."

With such instructions as these, perhaps it was not surprising that so many people were unwilling to change their beekeeping ways. But why were people apparently so slow in recognising that bees were good rent payers? Basically, there were two reasons. First of all there was usually little, excepting the innovator's enthusiasm, to commend one hive against another, and the old skep system often produced plenty of swarms but not much honey; a lot was left to chance. Secondly, working with bees requires a little more dedication and interest than the desire to make a few pounds on the side. Without good motivation, eventual failure is almost inevitable.

However, there was certainly no doubt about Dr. Cumming's own enthusiasm, which amounted to a religious fervour, and it led him to some extravagent conclusions.

"Bees rarely fail to become acquainted with a kind and affectionate master... They do not for-get little acts of kindness shown to them, and rarely fail to show gratitude." On the subject of drones, he points out that... "The beautiful Creator has left no place for indolence... the bees accordingly turn them out to starve, or garotte them as they catch them. Do idle young men deserve better treatment?"

In the closing letter Cumming takes this moralising much further by openly preaching an apiarian homily to English cottagers. He urges his readers to readers to copy the bees by working hard. "It is not work and plenty of it that kills people, but worry." Loyalty was another lesson to be learned. They love a queen, "Whose sovereignty is motherhood, and whose service is perfect freedom. They detest your republics, and democracies and radicalism in all its phases." Further, he cites the bees' cleanliness, sympathy with the sick, and early rising, as examples to be followed. The benefits of fresh air, too - "My bees would die in a London bedroom in twelve hours." Finally, the radical reformer, John Bright, is put on the carpet. Bright was a pacifist who sought to disband the army, and Cumming ridicules this idea, saying, "LOOK at the bees and how sensible they are about beekeeping." Elsewhere, he draws similar conclusions about the troubles in Belfast.

Many of these sentiments found a ready ear amongst readers of **The Times**, but if they ever reached the ears of the cottagers, they were met with stoic indifference. The cottagers did not need a beemaster to tell them about hard work, or that their womenfolk should stay at home and work, not go about gossiping. Nevertheless, such beliefs were held quite sincerely by Dr. Cumming, and it is fascinating to see these social attitudes coming through in a simple book about beekeeping. Furthermore, it perhaps demonstrates that an indifferent text can sometimes be quite as interesting as a good one to subsequent generations.

What is surprising is that Dr. Cumming found a good publisher, Samson Low, for his book when throughout the history of beekeeping many important books have had to be published by the writers themselves, a venture not to be lightly undertaken at any time. So, if he does not quite come up to the mark as a beemaster, at least he made an impression in the publishing world, and he has left us with some interesting side-lights on the beekeeping of his day. In complete contrast, in Philadelphia, some twelve years earlier, an American clergyman had published one of the real masterpieces of beekeeping literature. The letters of Huber, and the work of Dr. Bevan had stimulated his interest to the subject, and in the next chapter we shall be taking a closer look at this man and some of his colleagues.

Chapter Seven

LANGSTROTH

From: "The American Beekeeper's Manual" (1850).

The American influence on beekeeping world-wide has been considerable, and it is almost impertinent to try to introduce even a few of their larger-than-life characters on so small a stage as this. Size, it is fair to say, is the essence of the American contribution, and just as Henry Ford showed the world how to set about mass producing motor cars, so did their beekeepers demonstrate how honey could be produced and marketed on a large scale. Likewise, their appliance makers developed new techniques and methods to serve an expanding industry.

Honey Production for a livelihood was more demanding than the keeping of bees by cottager or small farmer as a side-line, and many of the old fashioned ideas were eroded as scientific beekeeping gradually became established on both sides of the Atlantic, and commercial beekeeping grew into big business.

For many years, however, beekeeping had remained a largely neglected occupation. John M. Weeks, of Salisbury, Vermont, thought this was due to the fact that the wax moth had found its way to America from Europe, and had caused so much depredation. In 1836, he wrote a manual which was popular for about twenty years. It was a simple guide, perhaps too simple -("Bees in large hives never swarm") - and published with an eye to the sale of the author's

"Vermont Hive," Nevertheless, Weeks had kept bees since 1808 and had lost his entire stock four times before writing his book. So, in some respects he could claim to be writing "out of experience."

John Weeks was clearly a hard-working, honest beekeeper, and his little manual deserved its success. He was something of a philosopher, too:-

> " ... In short, the whole system of natural instincts of the bee magnifies the wisdom of their Creator. If human reason could be made to exhibit this perfection, we should have no more quarrels between rich and poor, or struggles between the subject and patronage and power. But all must be free to choose between right and wrong; and this has become corrupted and imperfect by moral depravity. May the time soon come when order shall be restored to the moral as it has aiways prevailed in the physical world."

It is rather a pity that Weeks seems to have been virtually forgotten in the same way as T. B. Miner .has been In 1849, Miner published "the result of many years experience" in a book called **The American Beekeeper's Manual**. Quite a different personality from Weeks, Miner was by no means over-modest, and he claimed that his book was a comprehensive treatment on the management of the honeybee. Hitherto, according to Miner, apiarians in the United States had been discouraged from producing a truly popular work because "the subject was too dry." He goes on to claim that his "success in the culture of this insect has been beyond precedent," and offers this work as worthy of the confidence of the public.

Rev. L. L. Langstroth

As with many of his European counterparts, with whose work Miner was familiar, there was certainly no lack of confidence. He had travelled through New York State and talked to all the beekeepers he could find there and, naturally, he had designed his own "Patent Equilateral Bee-hive" which was, of course, the final answer to every beekeeping problem! This valuable hive could be bought for five dollars, with a right to make further hives for the purchaser's own use; alternatively, the drawings, including the same right, could be bought for two dollars. Miner's pretentious claims enjoyed some limited recognition, but very soon the work of two or three other bee men was to lay the foundations not only of a new industry, but for an entirely new approach to beekeeping. Moses Quinby wrote **Mysteries of Beekeeping Explained** out of his experiences as a producer of ten tons of honey per year, and Lorenzo Langstroth's **The Hive and the Honeybee** had the same intellectual integrity as the work of Huber and Butler. Both these books were published in 1853, and they marked a watershed in American beekeeping, although Langstroth's influence later became world-wide. Both books were kept in print for many years by the revisions of eminent beekeepers of subsequent generations, There are several instances in the literature of beekeeping where successful titles have been kept alive by these means.

Quinby's book was revised by his son-in-law, L. C. Root, the distinguished son of the celebrated A. I. Root, founder of the supply firm and the magazine **Gleanings in Bee Culture** which began life in 1873 and attracted five hundred subscribers in its first year. Root's book, **A.B.C. of Bee Culture** was first published serially"in this magazine which also featured accounts of Root's own many experiments. A. I. Root also ran a column for forty-eight years in which he discussed a wide variety of subjects, including such topics as the evil of tobacco. He once offered a free bee smoker to any tobacco user who would abandon the habit. As we shall see later, much space in the magazines was devoted to arguments about patents, but Root, himself, who was always ready to discuss freely his own ideas and provide detailed instructions for making appliances, etc., was opposed to the granting of patents for beekeeping.

The first copy of a bee magazine in the English language however, appeared on 1st January, 1861, when Samuel Wagner, a bank cashier, produced **The American Bee Journal** some twelve years prior to the launch of **Gleanings**. A. I. Root was a contributor to the Journal for some years, and as Frank C. Pellett points out in his **History of American Beekeeping** he was one of many contributors who even,tually achieved a world-wide reputation. "The history of **The American Bee Journal** had been the history of the rise of beekeeping, and the one is inseparably linked to that of the other," wrote Pellett.

Moses Quinby

In 1863, a couple of years later, Charles Dadant settled in Hamilton, Illinois, from France. He was then forty-six, and could speak little English, although he had no difficulty in writing the language. By 1867, he had made he had made his first contribution to the **American Bee Journal** and had embarked on a long series of experiments with hives. Charles Dadant wrote extensively for both the **American Bee Journal** and European publications. He also took his son into partnership, and C.P. Dadant became as well known as his father. They established the business of beekeeping suppliers, and although Charles Dadant unfortunately did not live long enough to see it, (he died in 1902), their firm took over the publication in 1912.

The Dadants were by no means strangers to publishing because in 1885, Lorenzo Langstroth went to Illinois to see if Charles Dadant would help him to revise his book, **The Hive and the Honeybee**. Their common interest in the honeybee enabled Dadant, a free thinking liberal, and Langstroth, a devout churchman, to work harmoniously together. A little time before Langstroth's death, the Dadants took over the copyright and their business expertise, together with their extensive beekeeping experience ensured the continued success of this remarkable book right up to the middle of the twentieth century. Since 1946 **The Hive and the Honeybee** has been the work of a group of writers, and two of the Dadant family are among the contributors. The name of Langstroth is no longer included in the title, and the charm of those earlier editions has been largely overshadowed by technical expertise.

Now, it is no accident that the name of Langstroth is held with respect and affection, not only among his fellow countrymen as the "father of American beekeeping," but in countries throughout the world. Of course, there are a few cynics who say that Langstroth's achievements were of minor importance, even that his ideas were copied, but these are but a tiny minority. Most people, once they have read Langstroth"s work, succumb to his magnetic personality and warmth. Many of the great. bee books have this same quality, where the writers are able to communicate more than the mere expression of fact and opinion.

The urge to communicate seems to come naturally to many beekeepers, and although the work of people such as T, B. Miner sounds brash and over-confident to the modern ear, there can be no doubt that such writers were usually very sincere and genuine people. With Langstroth, communication had an almost evangelical quality, and it comes as no surprise to find that, like so many other writers on bees, Langstroth was a parson. He possessed an almost mystical aura, or at least something more than a comprehensive knowledge of bees, which earned him the respect and devotion of such strong characters as A. I. Root and Charles Dadant. It is significant that Dadant, who certainly posessed the ability and experience to write such a book himself, was willing to undertake the revision of Langstroth's work. Also that Sam Wagner had earlier put aside his own manuscript in order to encourage and support the production of **The Hive and the Honeybee**. Under these circumstances of rare unselfishness, it is perhaps not altogether surprising that this book has sometimes been said to be one of the most influential books in beekeeping. Langstroth was clearly a most extraordinary man, although his life was dogged by poverty, ill-health and troubles of one sort and another.

Lorenzo Langstroth graduated from Yale in 1831, and became a tutor in mathematics. For some years he was principal of a "female academy" in Massachusetts. He was ordained in 1836, and it was about this time that he took up beekeeping, an interest which was to dominate his life for the next sixty years. He was nearly eighty-five when he died.

It is perhaps remarkable that, in a country which is noted for doing things on a large scale, Langstroth himself never seems to have kept more than one hundred and twenty-five colonies of bees. He was a breeder and importer-of queens - a pioneer in fact - and', of course, he studied. His library grew, and he taught himself to read French for the sole purpose of reading works on bees in that language.

Eventually, Langstroth came to the conclusion that what was needed was a hive so constructed that every part of its contents might be easily examined without due disturbance or damage to the bees. The basis of this, of course, proved to be correctly spaced moveable frames, and Langstroth is usually credited with this invention. Certainly it was largely this concept which revolutionised beekeeping throughout the civilized world, and whilst some of the ideas which Langstroth used may have been around for quite a time,

it was Langstroth who was able to sort the wheat from the chaff, and he was certainly not the kind of man who would wittingly steal the ideas of others. His reputation as the Huber of America was not built by publicity, although it was undoubtedly enhanced by the fact that Roots' mass-production methods and business efficiency did much to establish the Langstroth hive,

It is sometimes suggested, that Langstroth's original hives were made from discarded champagne crates, and this may possibly account for the fractional dimensions of his frames in inches. Whether this is so, or not is of little of little consequence, although these crates were made from substantial planed timber, which thrifty people would certainly have put to good use.

Prior to Langstroth, American -beekeeping had been in a very depressed state, "entirely neglected by the mass of those most favourably situated for its pursuit." It needed an articulate and intelligent leader, capable of transforming the archaic practices of the past into a coherent, scientifically well-founded system. Langstroth was the right man in the right place at the right time, and he fulfilled this role admirably. Very soon his influence spread into other countries, especially France, Italy and Russia.

In the years between 1873 and 1890, no less than 800 patents were filed in respect of beekeeping appliances in the U.S.A. It says much for the Langstroth hive, - (and perhaps the Roots' sales techniques) - with its simplicity and fairly large capacity that it became the one most widely used. During these years, however, the question of size was a fiercely debated issue, and at some stage even the Langstroth frame was altered from seventeen and three eighths inches to seventeen and five eighths inches. The editor of **The Beekeeper's Review**, W. Z. Hutchinson, a large scale operator from Michigan, refused space in his magazine for Charles Dadant to discuss the large hive because he was convinced that Heddon's contracted hive was the better proposition. With the market expanding, it is not difficult to see how important it was for the appliance makers to back the right horses! Hutchinson, incidentally, dedicated his excellent book to the beekeepers who earned their bread and butter from bees, and he did a great deal to encourage the expansionist philosophy.

It was the world of commerce, however, which caused Langstroth a good deal of unhappiness. He was not cut out for business in any way, and the patent he took out in 1852 caused him endless trouble. He sold the patent to agents and manufacturers up and down the country, but there were widespread infringements and disputes. There were legal proceedings, but Langstroth's case was not good enough to stand up in court and this, together with the financial strain, led to a complete mental and physical breakdown in 1873. He was even obliged to give up his apiary. Fortunately, thanks to the kindness of friends, he was able to start up again later.

Actually, Langstroth had suffered from bouts of mental illness from the age of twenty. They sometimes lasted for several months, and he would be unable either to write or talk about the things which had delighted him when he was in good health. His friend, A. I. Root has described him as "a wonderful talker, as well as writer -one of the most genial, good-natured, benevolent men the world has ever produced." He had a fund of anecdotes, and the gestures of a man caught up in a zest for living.

One day, he had a difference of opinion with Root in the latter's apiary. They argued with some heat and bitterness. In the end Langstroth took him by the arm and said: "Friend Root, will you not forgive me? I have been rude and uncourteous. You have practiced this thing, and are succeeding. Very likely you are right, and I am wrong." There seems to be no evidence to show what the dispute was about, but Langstroth's conciliatory tone is worth noting. Perhaps it was to do with the alteration in the size of frame.

A. I. Root

In his later years, Langstroth liked to visit Root, and one evening the conversation turned towards the troubles over the patent. Root knew that the subject tended to depress the old man, and he gently tried to turn his mind to the christian belief of doing good towards them that hate you, and so on. But Langstroth became depressed and morose, and retired early to bed.

In the morning, fearing the onset of a severe bout of depression, Root went to Langstroth's bedroom. The old man was awake, and he took his watch from under the pillow.

"Listen! Root, listen to what that watch is saying."

Root, who had once been a watch-maker, thought there must be some ir regularity in the movement, but he could find nothing wrong. He felt sure Langstroth was going out of his mind.

"Mr. Root," he continued, "that watch has been saying '-'Quinby! Quinby!

Quinby!" all night long, and I can't stand it any longer. I am going to start out to-day; I am going to see Mr. Quinby. I am not going to say a word about the patent or about the hive. I am going as though we had always been friends."

Langstroth went to see Quinby, and the two men were said to have "had the best time in the world."

It may be fair to say that Langstroth was more of an academic than most of his beekeeper contemporaries. Education may have helped him with the evaluation of evidence, and the way in which inventions were presented, but it does not explain the uncanny warmth and friendliness which permetes which permeates through every page of **The Hive and the Honeybee**. Unlike many earlier writers, he is frank and down-to-earth. He does not expound about his own abilities and uniqueness, but instead says things such as: "Before terminating this comparatively short, but perhaps to many of our readers, tedious study of the organs of the bee, etc." In fact, Langstroth is very rarely tedious, although it was entirely natural for him to introduce religious references into his work:

> "I would, however, utterly repudiate all claims to having devised a perfect bee-hive. Perfection belongs only to Him, to whose omniscient eye were present all causes and effects . . . when He spake, and from nothing formed the Universe. For man to stamp the label of perfection upon any work of his own, is to show both his folly and presumption,"

Elsewhere Langstroth, like Swammerdam earlier, speaks about "investigating the works of God," and there can be little doubt that religion was the mainspring of all his endeavours. To the younger Dadant the religious overtones struck a somewhat discordant note, but they were nevertheless largely retained in later revisions out of respect for Langstroth. The modern reader may be surprised to find so strong a spiritual force in a man whose interests were essentially scientific, and perhaps be impressed by his often uncommonly vivid descriptions. Of a queenless colony, he wrote:

> "Their home, like that of a man who is cursed in his domestic relations is a melancholy place, and they enter it only with reluctant and slow-moving steps."

How is it possible to sum up this larger than life individual, this man whose face had such honesty and good humour? His talents were many, but they failed to save him from the snares of commerce. He had good friends, but they were unable to protect him from the ruthless exploitation of others. Fate, too, turned against him when, at the height of his troubles, he lost a good wife, and an only son. Lorenzo Lorraine Langstroth has been described as "the Huber of America," and it is doubtful if anyone will ever improve on that description.

The latter half of the nineteenth century was probably one of the most interesting periods in American beekeeping history, and it is a pity that Frank C. Pellett's excellent book which deals so well with this subject, is so difficult to obtain. In the 1880's, for example, great strides were made in the raising of queens on a commercial scale, first by Henry Alley and later by G. M. Doolittle, who introduced a system of dipping artificial cells by means of a wooden stick placed in melted wax. As for large-scale beekeepers, Moses Quinby, whom we discussed earlier, had some 1,200 hives at one time, and one of Quinby's disciples, a Capt. J. E. Hetherington, of New York, was reckoned to be the largest beekeeper in the world with some 3,000 colonies. Incidentally, it was the sugar shortage during the Civil War which really put Quinby on his feet as a major honey producer, and he is generally thought of as the father of commercial beekeeping in the States. But the size is by no means everything, and in the next chapter we shall take a look at a few more American and British beekeepers, some of whom worked on quite a modest scale. Nevertheless, it was this new energy and enthusiasm from widely differing sources which helped to forge the beekeeping we know to-day.

Charles Dadant

Chapter Eight

QUICKENING PACE OF CHANGE

From: "Scenes of Industry" (1827)

Some families enjoy a tradition of beekeeping, where skills and enthusiasms pass from one generation to another, but it often happens that great beekeepers become so almost by accident. A. I. Root has described how his interest in bees was awakened by the sight of a swarm; Langstroth by the sight of a jar of cut-comb honey, and so on. As we mentioned in the last chapter, Root was originally a jeweller and watchmaker, and Umgstroth a mathematician, teacher and minister. Dr. C. C. Miller, another pioneer, had been a teacher and an organ salesman, before he devoted his life to beekeeping in Illinois. All these men became respected authorities in the United States, and were largely self-taught in so far as the practical and scientific aspects of beekeeping were concerned.

As interest in beekeeping grew, colleges of education responded accordingly and more formal text-books were written. In 1876, for example, A. J. Cook, professor of entomology in the Michigan State Agricultural College published, **Manual of the Apiary** later known as **The Beekeeper's Guide**, a highly successful manual which dealt systematically with both the natural history of the honeybee and apiary management. This interest by educationalists was, of course, by no means confined to the U.S.A.

In this country, for example, Frank R. Cheshire, a lecturer on apiculture at South Kensington, produced **Bees and Beekeeping: Scientific and Practical** in two volumes. This. ambitious work, originally published in parts, ran to almost a thousand pages, and created quite an impression on both sides of the Atlantic. Later editions of Professor Cook's **Manual** contained several references to Cheshire, a sign that communication between beekeepers was improving. Although Cheshire's book is impressive, critics have pointed out that he borrowed heavily from other sources without acknowledgement.

It is not easy to assess quite how fair such criticism is because most writers tend to be avid readers, and normally take some account of previously published material. Most writers are only too anxious not only to give credit where other peoples' opinions are cited, but often to dedicate their work to those who have helped and inspired them. Professor Cook, for instance, gratefully dedicated his manual to the Rev. L. L. Langstroth.

Dr. Miller was another who freely acknowledged the help he had received from A. I. Root, Moses Quinby and' other contributors to the **American Bee Journal**. In 1894, Miller himself, at the age of 63, took over the job of answering correspondents' queries in the **A.B.J.** What a fascinating, friendly man Miller was! His father, also a doctor, had died when he was ten, but despite extreme poverty, C. C. Miller went on to gain admission to Michigan University where he, too, qualified as a doctor.

For about a year (1856), Miller practiced medicine, but he was so apprehensive that some error of judgement on his part might seriously affect the life of a patient, that he decided to give up his profession. For a time, he taught music, and at about the age of thirty, he began to keep a few stocks of bees with the help of Quinby's **Mysteries of Beekeeping Explained**.

Dr. C. C. Miller

Miller first met Root in 1870, and showed him how to use rotten wood for smoking bees, and Miller later recalled that first meeting and how Root had seemed very pleased with his new smoker, despite the fact that he set fire to the first hive he used it on! No doubt both men would scarcely have credited that Root would have sold three hundred thousand similar smokers by the turn of the century. Beekeeping was certainly well on the way to becoming big business!

Hard-selling was nothing new in beekeeping, of course, and many books had been written by those with hives to popularise, or systems which they thought would be trouble-free and profitable to user and inventor alike. C. C. Miller was of rather a different mould, and he was one of the first writers who communicated on a beekeeper to beekeeper basis, rather than as a master to his apprentice. Experiences were to be shared, and mistakes candidly admitted. Miller first wrote a little book under the title **A Year Among Bees** and later enlarged it as **Forty Years Among the Bees**. Finally, at the age of eighty, he enlarged it once again as **Fifty Years amongst the Bees**. There are no chapter headings; the book flows along in friendly conversation from one topic to another, and the reader is able to share the joys of this deeply religious man as he gradually comes to terms with the ups and downs of keeping bees. Beekeepers certainly enjoyed his writing, but whether one English critic was fair to say that "he earned more by his writings than ever he did as a beekeeper," is open to doubt.

Prof. A. J. Cook

Commercial development by appliance dealers was not confined to America, of course. In England, George Neighbour and Sons had been established in Holborn since 1814, and the firm had been helped on its way when Thomas Nutt offered it the agency for the Collateral and other hives in 1824. Neighbour's son,. Alfred, often accompanied Nutt on visits to the firm's customers. The Neighbours maintained a public Apiary at Regent's Park Zoo until it was taken down to make room for a monkey-house. They were also friendly with Henry Taylor, author of the **Beekeeper's Manual**, who lived at Highgate. The firm continued to prosper until well into the 1890's.

John Milton was another Victorian appliance dealer, to whom reference was made in chapter VI. In fact, by the 1870's, hive makers were springing up everywhere, and one of the most flamboyant was Captain Piers Edgcumbe Martin, a retired sea captain, who established "The Great Hampshire Bee Farm," near Stockbridge. He invented the Sailor's bee-hive which he rashly claimed was the standard bar frame hive for the United Kingdom. As with many others this enterprise did not last, and the Sailor's hive slipped into oblivion. On the other hand, Robert Lee of Uxbridge was established in 1862 and this firm has survived. Similarly, in Scotland about ten years or so later, young Robert Steele, living at Fowlis Easter in Angus started the firm of Steele and Brodie. Continuing for a moment on the subject of appliance dealers, E. H. Thorne, once an estate foreman and a ship"s carpenter, started to make beehives in Lincolnshire in 1910 .

T. W. Woodbury

T. B. Blow

Credit for the first British moveable frame hive in 1861 usually goes to T. W. Woodbury, of Exeter, and there is an excellent account of this remarkable beekeeper's work in R. H. Brown's **One Thousand Years of Devon Beekeeping**.

George Neighbour with son, Alfred

Thomas Woodbury was only 52 when he died, and his achievements generally seem to have been under-rated, perhaps because he did not write a book. Nevertheless, Woodbury wrote about bees in horticultural magazines, and he had correspondents all over the country, including Charles Darwin. On 3rd August 1859, he probably became the first man to import a queen into this country when a rough deal box containing about a thousand Ligurian bees arrived from Switzerland. (It is said, incidentally, that he taught himself German so that he could study the writings of Dzierzon and others).

Three years later, Woodbury's yellow bees attracted the attention of visitors to the International Exhibition, and under the auspices of George Neighbour and Sons, he exported four stocks of these bees to Melbourne. The journey took seventy-nine days from 25th September, and the bees were said to have thrived in their new environment.

Neighbour and Sons were also involved in 1879 with the first import of Carniolan bees in conjunction with the Rev. W. C. Cotton, as mentioned earlier. Cyprian bees were first brought in by T. B. Blow some years later, but just as the Carniolans went out of favour because of excessive swarming, so did the Cyprians fail to please because of their irascibility. T. B. Blow, incidentally, founded the firm of Taylors, at Welwyn, in 1887; he was a man who spent much of his time abroad, in the Middle East, the U.S.A. and Japan. From one of his trips to the latter country, he brought back a Japanese wife.

The appliance industry continued to expand, helped by the new inventions which were naturally good for trade. Thanks largely to Langstroth, and the publicity of the appliance manufacturers, now that it was possible to remove frames from a hive at will, the tide was on the turn. It is interesting to note, however, that Neighbour wrote of Woodbury that he was, "with the ordinary bar frames so exceedingly expert a manipulator that he could not perceive any advantage over moveable bars!"

The Great Exhibitions in 1851 and 1861, as well as the Crystal Palace shows later, stimulated enormous interest, and the beekeeping industry was not slow to take advantage of such publicity on a large scale.

Ideas flowed in from America. H. O. Peabody manufactured the first extractor, or "honey-slinger" for sale in 1870, and others quickly followed. The first "honey-slinger" to be sold in England was made by R. R. Murphy of Illinois, but the price of £8 delivered was too expenstve and British manufacturers began to market their own. T. F. Bingham is generally credited with the design of the first. really practical smoker, although both A. I. Root and Quinby had very similar ideas. In about 1892, E. B. Weed, of New York, devised a process for the mass production of wax foundation. Another introduction from Illinois solved a problem to which British beekeepers such as Cheshire had found no really satisfactory solution, and this was the bee escape which was in introduced by E. C. Porter in 1891.

The upsurge of interest in the latter half of the nineteenth century was, of course, by no means an over-night affair. Beekeepers tend not to be easily persuaded, and despite the changing climate many remained naturally sceptical about yet more wonderful systems and new fangled ideas. Apart from this, the working classes had very little money to spare. In 1870, the Education Act was passed, and the age of popularisation was beginning. The wonders of nature were being exploited for the newly literate, and the books by Sir John Lubbock, and the Rev. J. G. Wood, were the expression of a new awareness of insect life, especially in relation to bees. A few years earlier there had been Samuelson's book on the "microscopical beauties" of the honeybee, and in 1866, W. E. Shuckard's **British Bees**, although not a work of this kind, nevertheless contributed to the natural history of the bee in the same way as William Kirby's had done some sixty-four years earlier.

Yet,despite these scientific advances, which was probably the most popular book of the period? It was published in 1870 and remained very popular for more than twenty years, and was the work of a professional gardener named Pettigrew. He freely acknowledged that **The Handy Book of Bees** was simply an exposition of the methods practised by his father, which he himself, "the bee-man's son" had followed for forty years. That system was based on the use of a skep of larger than usual size. The Stewarton and other new bar-framed hives, as well as the American honey-slinger had many shortcomings, according to Pettigrew, and he certainly did not see much future for them. "How any sensible honest man can advocate wood for beehives is a marvel to me," he wrote. Nevertheless, Pettigrew was an honest, sensible man, and undoubtedly an able beekeeper.

In the very wake of Pettigrew's success, a man from Sussex published **A Modern Bee Farm** in 1887, in which he said:

> "It is sheer folly to suppose that a given swarm of bees will store just as much surplus honey in a common skep . . . as they will in a properly constructed modern hive ... "
>
> "Moveable frames-large frames and large hives admit of such manipulation that a given swarm may yeild four or five times as much as it would do in a skep, or makeshift hive".

This man was Samuel Simmins, a small farmer whose idea of beefarming was that bees on their own were not sufficient to provide a living and that other forms of livestock should be kept, and crops should be grown. The whole enterprise should be subservient to the bees, of course, although fruit growing and clover crops, for example, would obviously benefit considerably from the bees' activity. Thousands of copies of his book were sold in various forms, and later it achieved a fresh lease of life when war-weary soldiers of World War I, seeking a quiet life on a few country acres, found the optimism and enthusiasm of Samuel Simmins just the stuff upon which to feed their dreams. Just how far the variations of **A Modern Bee Farm** went may be judged from the fact that the first edition ran to 195 pages, and the last (1928) edition contained 506 pages.

Samuel Simmins

He was quite a prolific writer, publishing a pamphlet on the direct introduction of queens in 1882, followed by **Simmins' Non-Swarming System**, in 1886, and **Plumping, or Rapid Increase in Spring**, a few years later. In 1898 he started a quarterly review, entitled **Bee Chat**, but like the novel Mysticus, which he wrote under the Pen Name of "Mark Thyme" , this was not a success.

The name of Simmins became a household word amongst beekeepers, partly because of the advertisirig he did for the "Crown Heather Queens" which he marketed from "The Great Sussex Bee Farm" at Seaforth in the 1890's, and the celebrated "White Star Italians", which were produced at Heathfield from about 1914. He was said to have been a shy and retiring man, and his "upright figure and alert manner" apparently did not figure anywhere in the beekeepers' organisation which grew up in his lifetime. He had nine children and was very happily married for fifty years, until his death in 1940 at the age of 83.

A man bursting with energy and brimful of confidence, Simmins had his own ideas about most things, including health, and his boast was that he had not consulted a doctor in fifty years. "The application of bee-stings" (as a cure for rheumatism) "is on a par with the barbaric practices of leeching and bleeding ... It is useless hoping to permanently cure local affections while the seat of the trouble - the digestive system - is neglected. The patient should be restricted to a temperate diet and the use of. honey instead of common sugar." It is not clear whether his book had much of a sale in America, although the style and even the spelling is Americanised, but his "White Star" breed of Italian queens were certainly used by beekeepers in Kentucky and Massachusetts. He was also an avid reader of **Gleanings**, the Roots' magazine, and his approach to marketing was certainly American.

Honey producers at that time had reason to be worried about glutting the market and the low prices then prevailing, but Simmins had plenty of ideas about selling honey to show a reasonable return. He himself had put an observation hive, "with stores, brood and a nice yellow queen with the bees" in a grocer's shop window, exchanging it as soon as the brightness began to wear off. His honey label bore a notice saying:

> "I guarantee this honey to be quite pure and free from the usual impurities of old fashioned strained honey. This is "extracted" from the combs (without being broken in the least), by the aid of centrifugal force; hence its superior quality...
>
> ...(Signed)"

So far as beekeeping was concerned, it was obviously desirable to use the Simmins' "Conquerer" hive, along with the many other appliances such as the Simmins' self acting syrup feeder, Simmins' Simplicity or Makeshift Rack and so on. He also eventually marketed his own "B-well" remedy for Isle of Wight disease; but, to return to the hive, Simmins fayoured the use of a large frame, as did the Americans. Many other beekeepers preferred a smaller frame, although at least one of the leading beekeepers of the time agreed with Simmins. This was a Dublin born man named Charles Nash Abbott, and although the smaller frame was adopted as the British Standard, this question of hive design was to cause controversy for years, as indeed it sometimes does to this day. C. N. Abbott, who was a retired butcher, in fact played, an important part in the establishment of modern beekeeping in Britain, not least for his part in making the work of Dr. Dzierzon. the celebrated German beekeeper, available in English in 1882. (Dzierzon had discovered parthenogenesis in bees, reproduction without fecundation, some forty years earlier).

It was Abbot who had earlier launched the first British beekeeping magazine, **The British Bee Journal and Beekeeper's Adviser**, on 1st May, 1873. This monthly publication, although regarded initially as an educational medium, performed a vital service for beekeepers in many different ways. The success of this magazine was not really surprising because the need for it had been there for some time. It became bi-monthly after ten years, and in 1886 it was issued weekly, remaining so for many years. It has survived as a monthly, and retained its independent character. On the inauguration of the British Beekeepers' Association, Abbot himself became treasurer, and John Hunter, Secretary. The first general meeting ofthe B. B. K. A., was held at the Crystal Palace, Sydenham, on September 10th, 1874. Sir John Lubbock, [**Ants, Bees and Wasps**], was President, and among the committee members were F. Cheshire and the Rev. W. C. Cotton, to whom reference has already been made.

C. N. Abbot with "Little Wonder" Extractor.

Frank R. Cheshire.

Another member of the committee was T. W. Cowan, and -by December of that year, Cowan was clearly established as Chairman of the new organization. Few people at the time could have had any idea that T. W. Cowan would remain in office for the next forty-eight years. For better or worse, this was the long marriage which would help to forge the future shape of British beekeeping.

Chapter Nine
THE COWAN ERA

From: "The British Beekeepers' Guide Book" (1921 edition).

In **Blazing the Trail**, Leonard S. Harker describes a meeting of the Apis Club at Bristol in 1923. At this meeting Thomas William Cowan, who was Vice President, was 'awarded the club's first Gold Medal for his services to beekeeping for over half a century: "Mr. Cowan treated us to a most interesting history of the craft since 1873, at which time only about a dozen people used the moveable frame hive."

Was this, in fact, true, or was there a misquotation? Perhaps the point is not all that important because the formation of the B.B.K.A., was itself the signal for change, not only in beekeeping methods, but in education, organisation, representation and virtually every other aspect of the craft. As we have seen earlier, there had been several attempts to form beekeepers' organisations and all had failed. This time it would succeed; and to its chairman over those formative years must go much of the credit.

Who was this man who stepped on to the stage of British beekeeping just at the time when so much was about to happen? Thomas William Cowan. He was bom in Russia in 1840, the son of a Scottish civil engineer. The family was clearly very successful at business, and by the age of twenty-two, T. W. Cowan was the owner of the Kent Ironworks at Greenwich. He designed machinery for agriculture and engineering, as weU as being responsible for several sewerage schemes. In the eyes of the Victorians, as a man of ability, wealth and property, he commanded universal respect. The beekeepers knew instinctively that this young man of thirty-eight would make a good chairman, ready if necessary to put his hand in his pocket should the need arise, (which of course, it did!) and not a man who might be tempted to use the position for personal gain.

In 1881, Cowan published **The British Beekeepers' Guide Book**, a slim volume which ran into edition after edition right into the 1930's. It is interesting to make comparisons between the early and later editions of this book. In the first edition, we. find descriptions of such hives as "Abbott's Standard," the "Cheshire," and "Alexandra," the "Kilburn Collateral," and, of course, the "Cowan." In the twenty-fifth edition, we find the "W.B.C.," Taylor's "Dovetailed," Lee's "Holborn, and the only one remaining from the first edition was the "Cowan." (Naturally!) Incidentally, he also built up an impressive library, which was presented by the B.B.K.A., to the Ministry of Agriculture in 1928.

With Cowan's background in engineering, it was not surprising that he turned his inventive brain towards beekeeping appliances. He designed various types of extractor, including the first radial, which then sold at £1.50 to £2.50, against the American imports which were too expensive and did not sell all that well. Cowan was at pains to make clear that he, himself, had no pecuniary interest in the appliances which he designed, and which were made by Youngs of Perth.

In 1904 another book was published, which also became very popular, **The Practical Bee Guide** by the Rev. J. G. Digges, an Irishman. It survived in print until after the second World War, and is interesting in several different ways. Cowan claimed that Digges (pronounced "Digs," by the way) had infringed his copyright, and in due course Digges wrote an apology which was. apparently displayed for some time at B.B.K.A. Headquarters. The Irishman countered by claiming that Cowan had taken material from Cheshire's book in writing **The Honey Bee** (1890). Certainly, plagiarism is not unknown among the writers of bee books. There may have been some jealousy between Cowan and Digges, although the two men had far more in common than is generally realised.

In 1887, Cowan purchased **The British Bee Journal** and was active editorially for many years. Likewise, Digges was the founder of the **Irish Bee Journal** in 1901, and remained for many years its editor. Beekeepers were beguiled by the pleasant, almost poetic style in which Digges wrote, but he was a much more complex character than the simple, enthusiastic beekeeping parson he seemed to be. Like Cowan; Digges also had a number of business interests, including a creamery, a railway and a coal mine; so, it is not inconceivable that there was a sense of rivalry between the two men. Both men were subjected to criticism of a severe kind not generally associated with voluntary officials, although Digges did have the reputation of being rather a difficult man to get along with, and it is said that he did not keep any bees for the last twenty-five years of his life.

Rev. J. G. Digges

Cowan was an authoritarian figure, as R. O. B. Manley recalled in 1948: "I remember once at a meeting of the British Beekeepers'Association in London, while we were listening to a speech by one of the men on the platform, Mr. Cowan walked in late. To my surprise, the entire congregation rose to their feet and reverently remained standing until the great man had taken his seat - like the King opening Parliament. "

Manley, a man of independent views and a professional beekeeper, was one of Cowan's harshest critics. Writing some twenty years after Cowan's death, Manley felt that he had been responsible for the continued use of unprogressive methods in British beekeeping. Cowan's whole approach, of course, was that of the dedicated hobbyist, and he seemed to have no conception of what bee farming implied. According to Manley, Cowan was usually "depicted as manipulating 'his bees in an extremely impressive and dignified manner, while wearing a frock coat. But if you go in for bee farming, you will find that you won't want any frock coat, but a boiler suit, a pair of gloves and a veil."

In fairness to Cowan, there can be no doubt about the "ability, zeal and liberality which he cultivated and promoted the science and art of apiculture", to quote a well known beekeeper of the time.

Cowan's reception at that B.B.K.A. meeting confirms that this was amply recognised by his contemporaries, and it seems likely that some of his critics were ignorant of his immense contribution to beekeeping.

One of Cowan's closest associates at the turn of the century was William Broughton Carr, who in 1890 moved south from the Wirral, where he had kept bees for many years. Carr assisted Cowan in the editorship of both **The British Bee Journal** as well as the **Beekeepers' Record**, a monthly journal which had been started in Merseyside in 1882, and taken over by Carr in 1889. In 1890, Carr, who owned im engraving business in Liverpool, sold his interest in the **Record** to Cowan. The association of these two men lasted until Carr died in 1909, a partnership perhaps best remembered by the double-walled hive which Cowan designed, and was later modified by Carr. Despite much criticism, it seems probable that the "W.B.C." hive will survive its centenary - and not many beehives have done that!

In 1897, W. B. Carr attended the Royal show which was held that year in Manchester, and it was there thal he was particularly impre~sed by the work of the expert to the Lancashire Beekeepers' Association, a man named William Her-rod. If Carr had been fishing for talents to enhance and expand the B.B.K.A., he could not have cast his line in more promising water, after all it was his home territory! Just how strong a character he had found, even Carr could scarcely have realised at the lime. Cowan was away in America for several years at this period, but upon his return he found that William Herrod, along with his brother Joseph, older by three years, had gone to the capital to take up the post as expert to the B.B.K.A. Seldom can such an appointment have been more propitious. It was not all that long before the incredible William Herrod exerted such an influence over beekeeping in this country that to question his authority was akin to doubting the place of the monarchy.

William Broughton Carr

Joseph Herrod-Hempsall

William Herrod-Hempsall

But to try to understand William Herrod, it is necessary to go back to his boyhood in the village of Sutton-on-Trent, in Nottinghamshire. The family lived in a cottage, 'often flooded by the river Trent. "Our parents," he wrote, "though poor ... were rich in those sterling qualities which have made the English nation what it is." No sacrifice was too great to enable the two sons "to follow all those pursuits which educate and uplift, instead of those which degrade." The boys were encouraged to keep themselves occupied, rather than waste their time playing cards and dominoes in the village institute ... such tastes resulting in several of their schoolmates becoming 'habitual frequenters of the public house."

It is not easy perhaps to appreciate the social framework which existed at the time. Working class boys, like the Herrods, left school at the age of eleven or twelve, and unless they were ready to use what little spare time they had to educate themselves, they had little prospect of any life other than as poorly paid artisans. Modest capital was difficult to acquire so that many skilled and gifted people had not much chance of entering the professional or employing classes. Further removed still were the landed gentry and the titled, with their divine rights of endless leisure and affluence: a significant point in any consideration of the life of one of the most outstanding, if sometimes controversial, beekeepers of the period.

Country boys such as the Herrods accepted this rigid social structure without envy or complaint. For them, this was the natural order of things, and they recognised that they would only "get on in the world" by hard work, self-education, and by following the precepts of their good-living parents. In the confines of village life, with its grinding poverty and endless gossip, any sign of ambition was regarded with suspicion. The Herrods were known as "the bee fakirs," an epithet which William remembered with some bitterness forty years later in one of his books.

The boys established an apiary with the help of Mr. R. Mackender, and before long they were travelling the countryside in a pony and trap, earning money from "driven bees." (To avoid the trouble of. "sulphuring," skep beekeepers were often glad for someone to take away the bees from selected stocks by driving them from one skep to another, a simple task which usually took about fifteen minutes). Agricultural shows of the period often had a class in which beekeepers competed against each other in this skill, and which William often won in about three minutes!

William's first job was as a gardener's boy, and later he worked for John H. Howard, an appliance-maker. By the time he met Carr, William Herrod's reputation as a beekeeper and prize winner at shows was already considerable. Precisely how much Joseph contributed to this reputation is not clear, but the brothers enjoyed a remarkably close relationship, and this persisted right through their lives. Joseph appears to have been quite the opposite of his brother, avoiding the limelight; a quiet, friendly man who was also a Fellow of the Royal Entomological Society, and very capable.

By 1909, William had bought **The British Bee Journal** and The **Beekeepers' Record** from Cowan, and had become secretary of the B.B.K.A. Cowan himself was still very active during this period, and published **Wax-craft** (1908), an important little book about beeswax, and **The Queen Bee** a popular account of bee life which included a dissectible model illustrating the principal external and internal anatomical features.

Sometime between 1912, when William Herrod published **Producing, Preparing, Exhibiting and Judging Bee Produce** and 1915, when he published **Beekeeping Simplified** he changed his name to Herrod-Hempsall. His brother, adopted the same style, and even today, the name is remembered by beekeepers everywhere, often as 'errod-'empsall, as if there had been only one man. In a curious way, this conception may not be so far from the truth because the back-room figure of the reticent Joseph often seems like the shadow of the more embullient William, the talkative front-man. In fact, William Herrod-Hempsall eventually became known all over the country as a judge, lecturer and examiner - R. O. B. Manley took a test under him as a young man, and even the Herrod-Hempsall's mentor, Mr. Mackender forty years after their first association was examined by him.

William had very little tact, and his blunt speaking and extremely dry sense of humour did little to enhance his popularity. The Americans were certainly rather flummoxed when he visited them, along with his wife. Their hospitality was stretched considerably by the Herrod-Hempsalls' insistence that tea be taken every day at four, and continued complaints about the weather, especially the size of the hailstones! Yet, writing later, Herrod-Hempsall clearly sensed none of the bewilderment he had caused and spoke highly of the generous treatment he had received. In general, however, he was not enamoured of American beekeeping.

Partly, this may have been due to his intense patriotism, and an abiding sense of loyalty, especially to those who had shown faith in him. For example, he always spoke with deeply felt respect for John H. Howard and Broughton Carr, but particularly for Thomas William Cowan, the man whose intellectual quality and integrity acted like a guiding star for his whole career. Incidentally, this same sense of loyalty may help to explain his almost invariable preference for British made appliances, and so on.

So far as Cowan was concerned, great though his contribution to beekeeping was, he probably stayed much too long at the helm of the B.B.K.A. In this respect the Herrod-Hempsall brothers seem to have been his loyal henchmen. This is no place to delve too deeply into the affairs of any association, although most people nowadays would regard it an essential condition of health of such organisations that responsibility and power do not dwell in the hands of too few people for too long.

As mentioned earlier, Manley was always critical of those who seemed to have closed minds to the new ideas about beekeeping which were coming in from abroad. Herbert Mace was another interesting character who was clearly ambitious to contribute to the politics of beekeeping, but by 1929 he found himself expelled from the B.B.K.A. For the moment, however, there is one other matter concerning William Herrod-Hempsall which cannot be overlooked.

In 1931 he published the first volume of **Beekeeping New and Old Described with Pen and Camera**. This work, the second volume of which was published in 1937, can only be described as monumental. No beekeeper can ever have left so revealing a monument, not only of his prejudices and pleasures, but of the whole beekeeping scene of his day. Lord Methuen wrote a foreword to the first volume, and Lord Snell, born under identical circumstances in the valley of the Trent and educated contemporaneously at the same village school as the Herrods, to the second. Inside, William is shown demonstrating bees to King George V at the Royal Show, Chester, and there is even a small picture of the actual queen which the King saw. What further proof could be needed that the gardener's boy had, like Lord Snell, climbed by sheer merit to the top of the tree? More to the point, it must be said that **Pen and Camera** is one of the most comprehensive works ever published on Bees and Beekeeping. Naturally, some of the information has gone out of date, but no beekeeping library can be complete without a copy.

William Herrod-Hempsall had much in common with that dynamic crusader of the.nineteenth century, Robert Huish, also Nottinghamshire born. Like the Wildmans, too, they all had the showman's flair, drumming up excitement and controversy, often insensitive to the feelings of others, yet they enriched beekeeping in a way seldom matched by the more conventionally educated.

But what of Joseph Herrod-Hempsall? For years he worked as editor of the two journals, and in 1948 revised the 8th Edition of W. B. Webster's **The Book of Beekeeping**, a book for the amateur. Even this has found its way under William's name in the index to **British Bee Books** (1979). Influential though Cowan and his disciples may have been during this lengthy period in beekeeping history, they did not have the stage entirely to themselves, and in the next chapter we shall focus our attention on a few others who also made an impression on their times.

Chapter Ten

THE EARLY 20th CENTURY

Photograph of Maurice Maeterlinck

The future prospects of beekeeping can have seldom looked better than at the start of the twentieth century. The price of honey was too low for the producer, of course, ,but so were other prices, and they changed little from year to year. New methods promised better yields, as well as better quality, and at long last the benefits of organisation and technical education were gaining the upper hand over superstition and neglect. But, as many a beekeeper knows, just as the moment when everything seems to be set fair, and the temptation to anticipate a rosy future begins to take a firm hold, some quirk of climate or other twist of fate will all too quickly change the whole scene to one of gloom.

One beekeeper who was uncommonly sensitive, not only to the fluctuating fortunes of his bees, but also to his own changing moods. was the Belgian, Maurice Maeterlinck. His book, **The Life of the Bee** (1901), written when he was forty, was translated into many languages, and was one of the best-selling bee books of all time. The reasons for its success were twofold: it was published at a time when literacy and interest in natural history were growing rapidly, but more especially it touched on a chord which had long fascinated people of a philosophical turn of mind. The relationship of **The Life of the Honeybee** to the life of man and the organisation within the hive were seen as a means of understanding man's place in the universal scheme of things. Even for a beekeeper like Maeterlinck, with some twenty years' experience, such an approach is difficult to sustain, and it becomes all too easy for fancies to overwhelm facts. Maeterlinck was probably the last serious writer to try to develop these ideas, and although he cut little ice amongst working beekeepers, his work nevertheless appealed to a very wide audience.

Nowadays, he is regarded as little more than a curiosity, and his high-flown language, whilst good enough to win the Nobel prize for literature in 1911, and for the writing of successful stage plays, now seems curiously archaic and remote.

> "In proportion as a society organises itself, and rises in the scale, so does a shrinkage enter the private life of each one of its members. Where there is progress, it is the result of a more and more complete sacrifice of the individual to the general interest ... "

Materlinck said that he had read "almost all the books on bees," and' in his **Life of the Bee** he simply tried to share the love and wonder which he himself had experienced. He made numerous experiments and observations with the intention of later writing a technical book, but this intention does not seem to have been realised, although he did write other books on insects before he died in 1949.

Sometimes his poetic instincts led him remarkably near to truths which have only been fully established in more recent times. When Maeterlinck discusses "the spirit of the hive." he comes very close to describing pheremones, or queen substance, and its effect on the bees' activity. His descriptions of swarming are clothed with extravagant language which certainly conveys the, excitement of the exodus, but 'practical beekeepers find the translation of these happenings into human terms somewhat embarrassing. It is precisely this quality, however, which often appeals to the general reader who can best relate to emotions and logic which are familiar to him. Later in life he wrote a book about ants which was far less intense and theatrical.

Maurice Maeterlinck was the son of a wealthy Belgian landowner. He began his career as a lawyer, but by the age of twenty-seven, having lost virtually all his cases, he gave up the law. He was a man who shrank from society, and spent much of his time in a world of conjecture and dreams. The use of the symbolism of simple things to give expression to philosophical ideas helped to draw attention to his writing, although his growing fame as a writer seized him with panic and terror. "All ceremony alarms me. I am a peasant," he protested.

Relaxation after writing for Maeterlinck was to work in the garden, and attend to the bees. He never seems to have been concerned about Honey

Production, as if to handle and observe the bees was in itself reward enough.

Herbert Mace

Rev. E. Tickner Edwards

Despite his dreamy nature, he was a man of solid build, and he liked manual work. He did his own car repairs, for example, and at one time he was a member of the Civic Guard. "Your epistle arrived this afternoon while I was out in the country getting my bees into winter quarters. I came home very late, and as I have an inspection of arms in the morning, I have still got to clean my Guard's musket,"

How is it possible to sum up this taciturn, pipe-smoking beekeeper, whose play, **The Blue Bird** captivated audiences throughout the world? On the one hand, he seems to personify the noblest virtues which are sometimes attributed to beekeepers. Yet on the other, he was an authority on gambling and the breeding of dogs, and sometimes there is a violence and brutality in his work which belies the concept of a man of contemplation and peace. His description of the massacre of the drones, for example, dwells heavily on every aspect of physical violation. But much worse is his essay, **The Massacre of the Innocents**, which is little moe than a sickening catalogue of bloodshed and bestiality.

If the complexities of Maurice Maeterlinck were somewhat out of tune with cottage beekeepers of the period, an English country parson was soon to provide them with an alternative. The Rev. E. Tickner Edwardes began writing about bees for the **West Sussex Gazette** and **Bees as Rent-Payers** was the first of a number of successful books. In fact, Tickner Edwardes was probably one of the most popular writers on bees in the first half of this century, and although **The Times** found his, **The Lore of the Honeybee**, "not unworthy to rank beside the masterpiece of Maurice Maeterlinck," the two men had little in common.

Another critic thought that Edwardes's book had "all the virtues of Maeterlinck's well-known prose epic, without its failings." Authors with the ability to "preserve the perfume of country joys in printer's ink" enjoyed particular success at this time. S. L. Bensusan, for example, was another rather whimsical writer on country themes who published a children's book about bees in 1909.

The opening sentence of Tickener Edwardes, **The Bee Master of Warrilow**," will perhaps be sufficient to indicate the flavour of much of his work.

"Long, lithe and sinewy, with three score years of sunburn on his keen, gnarled face, and the sure stride of the mountain goat, the Beemaster of Warrilow struck you at once as a notable figure in any company."

Whether Edwardes himself is particularly notable as a beekeeper is another matter. He wrote about bees for the small-holder, and from his own long experience as a beekeeper. As such, he was influential over a considerable period, as indicated by his **Beekeeping for All** which first appeared in 1923, and remained in print for several years after the Second World War.

As we have seen earlier, this situation is very common in beekeeping, due to the longevity of so many beekeepers who remain active long after others have retired, or "passed to the great beyond," as HerrodHempsall would have said.

For example, in 1900 a young man named L. E. Snelgrove started to keep bees, as did Annie D. Betts, and in the Sussex of Tickner Edwardes, also a man named J. C. Bee-Mason. In the years which followed, all three were to make their marks in beekeeping at various times. Bee-Mason possibly became better known as an antarctic explorer (he was a member of Shackleton's expedition). He was one of the first people to make films about bees; in 1912 he made **The Life of the Honeybee** and two other films in the following year. He imported large quantities of Dutch bees in 1914, probably as a result of disease which was causing havoc amongst the country's bee stocks. It was this scourge, incidentally. that caused another young man, who started beekeeping in March 1915, ` to have serious doubts as to whether the apiary where he had started to work would survive the season. His work at Buckfast Abbey became known throughout the world over many decades, although it was 1974 before Brother Adam found time to write a book about his beekeeping methods.

"The scourge," of course, was Acarine, popularly known as "Isle of Wight disease," because it was on that island in 1905 that the disease assumed epidemic proportions. Although many beekeepers were not happy about it, the name of Isle of Wight disease has never quite been discarded. Furthermore, there are some aspects of this particular disease. which lasted so long, which continue to puzzle scientists even to-day.

Leaving aside these fine points of scientific difference, it is not always appreciated how seriously this disease ate into the heart of what promised to be one of the most progressive periods in beekeeping, and all but wiped out the strain of native dark bees which had hitherto done so well. In some respects, it is a sorry tale of muddle and indifference on the part of the authorities, but in others it represents a triumph for the small-time beekeeper and his persistent struggle to survive.

> Herbert Mace, recorded the following in his diary on 15th September, 1912: "Bees seen resting on alighting board, some trying to fly and unable to move; others crawling up stems and falling off. Many with one, sometimes both, secondary wings sticking out at an angle. Muday, yellowish excreta voided outside hives. Abdomen much swollen."

Before the end of January, all his seven remaining stocks had perished. "This was quite typical," Mace wrote later, "And it was no wonder that absolute panic prevailed ... the wisest thing to do was to destroy every colony as soon as symptoms appeared . . . no doubt many gave up keeping bees after several seasons fruitless battling with the dragon."

L. E. Snelgrove

Annie D. Betts

Because of the dysenteric symptoms, it was at first thought that the disease was a form of Nosema, and much time was spent investigating the bees' digestive system. Eventually, a beginner in beekeeping, Mr. A. H. E. Wood, who had lost five recently purchased stocks, financed research at Aberdeen University under a Dr. J. Rennie. By turning his attention to the breathing system, Rennie discovered that a parasite was damaging the tracheal walls of the bee. (Mr. Harrison Ashforth has described how a laboratory assistant named Elsie Harvey was actually the first to see the mite during a lunch time break). These findings were made known in a report to the Royal Society of Edinburgh in 1921. The parasite was named after Mr. Wood, ***Acarpis woodi***, and the disease given the scientific name of **Acarine**.

Later, in Switzerland, Dr. Morganthaler established that the mite could only enter the breathing tubes during the early days of the bee's life, a matter of nine days at most.

Diagnosis, however, is one thing, but treatment is another, and in the years which followed all kinds of cures were tried. Dr. Rennie, whose own health was failing, put forward several treatments, but the problem was to eliminate the parasite without destroying the bees, and it was not easy to solve. Success came, not from the great scientific establishment, but from a man who had taught himself beekeeping with the aid of Cowan's little guide book and, following his own losses, had bought equipment to learn about dissection and the use of microscopes. He was a man of limited means, finding that even the cost of sugar for feeding was really more than he could afford. This additional expense was quite a burden. His name was R. W. Frow, and he was the station master of Wickenby, eleven miles from Lincoln.

R. W. Frow

E. H. Thorne

Frow experimented with all kinds of substances, and eventually tried a mixture of nitrobenzine, safrol and petrol, used on a vapourising pad. Safrol was used at the time in the treatment of whooping cough, and nitrobenzine (oil of mirbane) as a constituent in sprays for domestic pests. The mixture was very cheap to make, although dangerous to handle because it was poisonous and highly inflammable.

On October 15th, 1927, he felt confident enough to send a sample of treated bees up to Aberdeen, where a Dr. Guy D. Morrison, had taken over Rennie's work. On the 17th October - (please note the speed with which both scientists and postmen worked in those days!) - Frow received his reply: "

> ... Your treatment seems to be most effective, and if it can be applied without doing the bees any permanent injury, it may be an epoch-making discovery in the control of acarine disease. We should be very pleased to have particulars of the treatment, and, of course, we should treat your method in strict confidence if that should be your desire."

But this quiet man from Lincolnshire, with no wish for publicity, and anxious to help his fellow beekeepers, published his formula and methods in **The British Bee Journal** of 17th November, 1927. He did not seek any other reward, although he was awarded the M.B.E., some nineteen years later.

On the other hand, Frow probably received the rewards he valued most. He had already gained the friendship of people such as E. H. Thorne, the appliance dealer of Wragby who had helped and encouraged his work, Dr. Morganthaler, the Swiss scientist, and Annie D. Betts, but most of all, the fellow beekeepers who continued to visit him until his death in 1973.

Nowadays, of course, there are other methods of dealing with acarine disease, which no longer poses the threat it once did. Modern text-books tend to remain silent about the Frow treatment. Nevertheless, despite the fact that care needs to be taken as to how and when it is applied, many beekeepers still swear by it.

Annie D. Betts discussed the Frow treatment, along with various modifications of it, in her book **The Diseases of Bees** (1934). She had published a book on bee anatomy some eleven years previously, and played a significant part in beekeeping during the period between the wars. During the First World War, she had been engaged on aeronautical research, and later published many articles in The **Bee World**, a magazine of which she was editor for twenty years, from 1929. Apart from beekeeping, she was a linguist, and a keen motor-cyclist and clearly something of a character in the home counties.

In 1919, just after the end of the First World War, she came under the influence of what must have been one of the most meteoric careers in beekeeping. An Egyptian doctor of medicine, A. Z. Abushady, formed a company in that year in Benson, in Oxfordshire. This company owned some two hundred hives, and traded in bee produce and appliances. Abushady had come to Britain as a medical student in the spring of 1912, at the age of twenty, and during the War had qualified at St. George's Hospital Medical School, London. Also in 1919, he formed an association of beekeepers called the Apis Club, and in addition started The **Bee World**. (Another successful magazine was also started by the Kent Beekeepers'Association a little earlier in the same year, known as **Bee Craft**. Ahmed Zaky Abushady was the first editor of The **Bee World** and one of his co-directors was Robert Lee, the appliance manufacturer from Uxbridge. Annie D. Betts has described the doctor as an international pacifist, and undoubtedly he saw the Apis Club movement as a vehicle for world-wide co-operation in beekeeping. He returned to Egypt in 1922, but in that incredibly short space of time, he had sown the seed for the organisation which was eventually to become the International Bee Research Association. The story of the early years of this organisation was covered in a book, **Bee Research Association, 1949 - 1974**, but there is one small comment which might perhaps be made here.

Beekeeping is not unique, of course, insofar as a great deal of voluntary work is done without any thought of personal reward, and how many times have old stagers watched enthusiasts, rather like Abushady, burn with incandescent brilliance for a year or two and then fade into nothing. On the other hand, there are others who give service year after year. Such a woman was Annie D. Betts, who kept **Bee World** going almost single-handed through the Second World War, finding that other people had no time. "I had none either," she wrote on giving up the editorship, when deafness was severely inhibiting communication with all but her closest friends and family. During those difficult years, a young woman with two honours degrees, named Eva Widdowson, had started to keep bees. That was in 1942, near Sheffield, and soon she was to marry and become future editor of **Bee World** and one of the major driving forces in the creation of the International Bee Research Association.

Before leaving the Apis Club, it is interesting to see that Dr. John Rennie became the first president in 1922. Apart from the foundation of an Apis Club by Dr. Abushady on his return to Egypt, the Apis movement found a ready response in other parts of the world. C. P. Dadant was a Vice President and both he and A. I. Root were to receive Gold Medals. In 1927, the Apis movement held its annual conference in Paris and delegates from many countries no doubt sampled the relativeiy new international flavour of their craft with some relish, although there was to be a great deal of hard work and some faltering before the world-wide organisation became a concrete reality.

Part of the early success of the Apis Club was due to the idealistic spirit which often thrives in the aftermath of a devastating war, when people are trying to find a more satisfying life-style. Leonard S. Harker, for example, was a wounded ex-serviceman who had also come under Abushady's spell in 1919. He saw the doctor as a man with a new vision of humanity, who had found the "galvanising instrument which will heal the sorrows of mankind." Harker played an active part in the early years of the Apis Club, and his **Blazing the Trail** published in 1938, provides an interesting insight into the world of Dr. Abushady and other beekeepers of the period. Amongst the long forgotten innovations put forward by Abushady was the use of artificial comb, made of aluminium or celluloid. Harker was friendly with R. O. B. Manley, who lived near Benson, also another ex-serviceman, Herbert Mace, both of whom are pictured in the book. Interestingly, the references to the HerrodHempsalls' are brief, but polite, although it is recorded that William visited Benson to wish Dr. Abushady "good-bye" in December 1922.

Robert Lee talking to Dr. Abushady at Benson, Oxon.

Herbert Mace, mentioned earlier, was a Londoner, and his early life was spent amongst bricks and mortar, with only rare opportunities to visit the country. At the age of twelve, he picked up some very cheap books on insects from a second-hand bookstall, and began to study natural history. Later, he moved to Epping, and in 1908, with the help of W. B. Webster's **Book of Beekeeping** he began his life as a beekeeper using some old hives bought in a sale.

Mace has written amusingly about his early experiences in Adventures with

Bees (1927), and these will strike a familiar chord amongst those who have trodden a similar path. He also provides us with graphic accounts of the anxieties and tribulations caused by acarine disease, and the efforts which were made to deal with the problem.

His first apiary was closed down as a result of the 1914-18 War in which he served as a soldier in the Balkans for three years. When he was discharged in 1919, his health wrecked by repeated attacks of malarial fever, he tasted the bitterness of a soldier's return.... "The newly discharged soldier seemed an interloper... and in my own case there has been a complete uprooting." His holding, with its spacious gardens and orchard had been replaced by an urban semi-detached house, with no more than a narrow strip of garden. "For the first year I resigned myself to bee-lessness."

Mace takes these set-backs without rancour, and he was typical of that breed of amateur beekeepers which abound in every generation, always ready to help and to share his knowledge with others. His writing has the same friendly atmosphere, and although he was essentially a populariser, he encouraged the use of charts and records. On one of his charts a honeyflow is plotted against cloud cover, wind, temperature, barometric pressure, etc.

For some years he published **The Beekeeping Annual**, which included features by Annie D. Betts, R. W. Frow, and Joseph Tinsley, the distinguished Staffordshire beekeeper who did research into queen mating and the wintering of bees. One of the ideas Mace had was to compile a directory of beekeepers, but from the five hundred questionnaires he sent out, only about a hundred and twenty-five appeared in the directory. Despite the notable omissions the list is of interest, although whether a popular writer on bees with only half a dozen hives of his own was tactful in attempting such an exercise is another matter. Mace's own entry ends with the cryptic words, "Expelled from B.B.K.A., by Council 1929." He does not give any explanation, although his critical survey of beekeepers' associations published in 1928 may have been partly responsible.

Herbert Mace continued to publish books for many years, and in 1937 appeared in the first television programme on beekeeping.

R. O. B. Manley was a man cast in a different mould, a professional in every way. He died in the autumn of 1977, at the age of-ninety, with a lifetime of beekeeping behind him. Manley is a fine example of a self assured, largely self-taught beekeeper, whose knowledge and wisdom extends beyond the common practicalities of his craft. He was a natural writer and to read his books is to joln him in the kind of leisurely conversation which might transpire amongst the hives after work on a summer's night. Manley had the precious gift of being able to see his own imperfections, and a sense of humour which rendered him devoid of any pomposity or false values. His attitude was that all knowledge is just the beginning, 'that even when the top of the mountain is reached, the plains ahead remain mysterious and unexplored. In a way, he had the powers of a story-teller, picking up threads from an enormous basket of experience and weaving them into patterns which were at once intelligible and illuminating.

Although Manley recognised that the climate and pasturage were far less favourable here than in some parts of the world, he was determined to prove that beekeeping was commercially viable. He never pretended that it was easy, and gives plenty of cautionary advice to those thinking of following in his footsteps. His main complaint was that beekeeping was orientated around hobbyists, and led by well-meaning, but often mistaken amateurs. This was no good for people who intended to produce honey as a paying proposition. Using the words of George Eliot, Manley writes - "The worst of all hobbies are those that people think they can get money at."

His first book, **Honey Production** (1936) caused quite a stir, but it immediately struck a chord amongst serious beekeepers. Manley took nothing for granted; he had a library of over three hundred books; he carried out his own experimental work and, steeped in knowledge from the past, he tested it against his own experience. He could not be ignored. Very quickly, Faber and Faber, the publishers, recognised his talent and took over the publication of his books. He wrote two others, both of which have become classics, as well as revising Digge's book and contributing to the bee press.

Robert Orlando Beater Manley - (what names to excite the curiosity!) never knew his mother, and this may have helped to shape his character. His colleague, Harry Wickens, has described how Manley often appeared rude to people when first introduced, whilst H. J. Wadey, for many years editor of **Bee Craft** has mentioned his chronic deafness, and the help and encouragement he had received from him. Oddly enough, Manley had an aversion to honey, possibly stemming from the time he was sick at the age of five, after having honey for tea at his grandfather's house. At twelve, he was found by his father' 'in a condition of coma in the ditch," after drinking a large glass of metheglin with a lady beekeeper! Neither experience affected him and at sixteen he had a few stocks of his own. An account of these early days is recorded by Manley with such warmth and affection that it is impossible not to enjoy his company.

Manley was born in 1887, only nine years after F. W. L. Sladen, but whilst Manley's heydays were in the thirties and forties, Sladen had made his mark and was dead by 1921. Yet the two men had quite a lot in common. They both earned their livelihood from bees, and they were both especially interested in American ideas, although perhaps not to the extent of condeming everything British which some beekeepers were inclined to do. Sladen endeavoured to popularise a strain of "Golden" bees, but they soon ran out of favour, and Manley certainly did not like them.

F. W. L. Sladen

R. O. B. Manley

But Sladen was more than a professional beekeeper, and his name deserves to be remembered for a number of innovations and observations. It was he who first described how the so-called wax pincers were used for packing pollen into the pollen basket [**corbicula**], and following the discovery in 1883 of the scent gland by the Russian observer, M. Nassanoff, it was Sladen, some seventeen years later, who was able to explain its nature and purpose. Nassanoff had suggested that it was part of the excretory function, but Sladen noticed the same scent from the abdomen of one of his freshly killed specimens. He went on to establish its purpose as a directional indicator, or perhaps more accurately, as an attractor.

Sladen had decided to make a living from bees at the age of 21, and has said that whilst he could have kept himself by Honey Production, it was only by bee breeding and queen-rearing that he could make enough money to bring up a family. In his book **Queen Rearing in England** there is a photograph of the Sladen home at Ripple, Dover, "built from the profits derived from breeding bees and queens in Ripple Court Apiary."

Most of Sladen's original work was published for the first time in the **British Bee Journal**, and his lecture on "**Mendelian Methods applied to Apiculture**" at the Zoological Gardens, London, on 10th September, 1912, was under the auspices of the B. B. K. A. (Mendelism, incidentally, was named after an Austrian Augustinian Monk, Johan Gregor Mendel, whose discoveries of the first laws of heredity were the starting point of the science of genetics in 1865. The significance of these discoveries were not fully appreciated until 1900 when three other scientists obtained similar results to Mendel).

Just as Mendel's work was virtually unrecognised in his own lifetime, it is perhaps fair to say that the value of Sladen's work was not fully appreciated until after his death. His book on queen-rearing has recently been reprinted, and his work on **The Humble Bee** remains a treasured classic. **The Humble Bee** was published in 1912, the year in which he emigrated to Canada. He lived there for about nine years, until his tragic death by drowning in a lake, where he was using island stations to conduct experiments on the mating of selected queens with selected drones.

Sladen's life had been devoted to bees, and at the age of sixteen he produced a stencilled treatise on humble bees. This brought him many friends,including naturalists such as Edward Saunders, author of **Wild Bees, Wasps and Ants**, (1907).

Another writer on queen rearing was L. E. Snelgrove, mentioned earlier. Snelgrove is best remembered for the three books which came out at roughly the same time as Manley's. His book **Swarming: its control and prevention** was quite popular, although some readers became baffled by the many alternatives which he provided. In this book, he described the "Snelgrove Screen board", a device which some beekeepers still find useful, although not very many. Manley described it as a "device intended for the amateur." His book on Roman bee lore was never published, and the work on queen introduction is thought by many to be his best. Altogether, these books are a wonderful testimony to Snelgrove's industry, for he gained most of his academic qualifications (he was an M.A. and M.Sc.) by working at night after a day's teaching in school, and at the same time became one of the most respected beekeepers of his day. Not surprisingly, Snelgrove held high office in several beekeeping organisations and became an inspector of schools.

Snelgrove kept bees in Somerset, Sladen in Kent, Manley in Oxfordshire; were there no celebrated beemasters in the north? Yes, of course, but an account such as this must inevitably be selective, and it must be remembered that every generation produces beekeepers who never put pen to paper, or look much further than their own locality. But, for the sake of balance, one or two names not associated with the south should, perhaps be mentioned.

There was John Anderson, for example, who wrote an interestmg obituary of Sladen in **Bee World** in 1921. He wrote many articles for British and American Bee Journals, as well as several papers on Isle of Wight disease, as a result of his involvement with the work at Aberdeen, where he lived. William Hamilton, another

Scotsman, was an extension lecturer in beekeeping at the West of Scotland Agricultural College, and later at Leeds University. He began beekeeping in 1906, and in 1945 published **The Art of Beekeeping**, a practical guide which helped the many newcomers to beekeeping at the end of the Second World War.

J. C. Bee Mason

John Anderson

Another Scottish beekeeper, born only about twenty years prior to John Anderson, will always be remembered for his part in assembling the library of the Scottish B. K. A., John Moir. Both Anderson and Moir kept only a very few hives, no more than half a dozen, which gives lie to the notion that only those who keep bees on a big scale have sufficient knowledge and authority to express any worthwhile opinions. Both these men were very knowledgeable and gave freely of their time in judging, lecturing and generally promoting the beekeeping cause. John Moil' was a pioneer trader, and he fought against the slave trade in Central Africa, a reminder, perhaps, that schoolmasters and clergymen are by no means the only articulate beekeepers.

Few men were more articulate than David Lloyd George, or George Bernard Shaw, although neither of them will enter the annals of beekeeping history by virtue of any contribution to the craft. Lloyd George inadvertently caused something of an uproar when showing his honey because there were strong suggestions that some judges were more influenced by his name than his produce, despite the customary anonymity of the show bench. Similarly, Shaw who was a frequent exponent on the virtues of honey, was at the eye of a storm because a fellow member of the County Wexford B. K., had proposed that his membership should be withdrawn on account of the blasphemous nature of his writing. The newspapers had quite a field-day on the subject in early 1933, using the analogies of stinging, swarming and so on to demonstrate their wit. It was a storm in a tea-cup for no action was taken. "One must congratulate them on their beelike wisdom," wrote one newspaper -"Not understood by too many societies and public bodies - in going back quietly to their work, which is the production of a useful commodity and not the chasing of heretics."

But beekeepers are unlikely to be impressed by this display of famous names. More likely they will ask, what happened to E. B. Wedmore, the electrical engineer, or Kelsey, Lawson, Stuart or Sturges... or indeed many another beekeeper who has provided enlightenment or entertainment in the first half of this century.

Then again, there are the living beekeepers and scientists whose longevity and service, invention and discovery, can match most of the great names from the past. But theirs is another story, beyond the scope of this modest essay, and one day - hopefully before they fade into the mists of time - this, too, will be told.

www.ingramcontent.com/pod-product-compliance
Lightning Source LLC
Chambersburg PA
CBHW081157270326
41930CB00014B/3183